STORIES FROM ANCIENT EGYPT

TITLES IN THIS SERIES:

MYTHS AND LEGENDS

STORIES FROM ANCIENT EGYPT

MARGUERITE DIVIN

Edited and translated from the French
by Barbara Whelpton

Illustrated by Daniel Dupuy

BURKE LONDON

First published in the English language September 1965

Reprinted October 1969

© BURKE PUBLISHING COMPANY LTD. 1965

Translated and adapted from *Contes et légendes de l'Égypte Ancienne*
© Fernand Nathan 1963

222   69227   8
222   69386   ×

BURKE PUBLISHING COMPANY LIMITED
14 JOHN STREET   ★   LONDON, W.C.1

SET IN MONOPHOTO BASKERVILLE
MADE AND PRINTED IN GREAT BRITAIN BY
WILLIAM CLOWES AND SONS, LIMITED, LONDON AND BECCLES

Contents

List of Colour Plates

I

The God Ra

REALLY magnificent palace was the earthly dwelling-place of the god Ra. Everyone admired the tall columns and obelisks which rose up on either side of the entrance; everyone marvelled too at the avenue which led up to it, for it was lined on either side by bronze sphinxes and stone lions.

On the immense gateways, fitted with huge bolts, was painted the image of the god Khonsu, the bull, whose task was to mount guard over the temple. Numerous servants were there also to protect the sun-god whilst he slumbered.

Ra, the sun, had only to open his eyes in the morning and it was dawn; in the evening, he closed them again and the shadows of the night darkened the earth. It was he, the golden hawk, who soared across the skies.

Each morning, on awakening, he was received by the two divinities of the East who surrounded him with respectful attentions. Then joyful sounds surrounded him as the women who dwelt in his palace greeted him with a song of good fortune, accompanied on musical instruments: "Awake in peace so that the goddesses of the crowns may also wake in peace. You bring joy, light and warmth to the earth!"

Once awakened, the god Ra went from his chamber into the cold baths and the daughter of Anubis, the goddess of coolness, arrived with her four pitchers of water, with which she showered the god. Then Horus rubbed his skin and Thoth dried his limbs.

Finally, Amon-Ra clothed himself again in his splendid robes and took his morning meal.

When he wished to go out, messengers set off at a run to clear a way for him; his courtiers formed themselves into two lines on either side of the route; and the soldiers of the guard bowed down until their foreheads touched the dust on the ground. Everyone lifted up both hands in adoration, crying: "All glory to you, god of the beings who gaze on your beauty!"

The barque of the god was waiting for him, moored to the river-bank: he embarked surrounded by the entourage of gods who were escorting him.

It was an enchanted ship, without oars, without sails and without a rudder, which glided over the waters of the skies; and, as it passed, both gods and men acclaimed their lord and master, the great god, Ra.

He followed his usual course around the world in this manner. Another ship took him towards Amantit, the mysterious region which is the Egyptian underworld.

Then leaving the earth, Ra penetrated into the nocturnal region by the Gate of the Corridors—a narrow cleft which cut the mountains in half—and disappeared from the eyes of men.

He continued to navigate the course of a great river whose valley was divided into twelve parts by walls and gates.

At each of the twelve hours of the night, the sun-ship passed from one zone to another. At the sixth hour, it crossed the northern frontier of the invisible world and came back to the Sacred Gate which leads to the Gardens of Ialou, where it arrived at the seventh hour.

Thus Ra, in his ship which had floated silently over the waters of the night, left these regions where the eyes of men could no longer follow him. He passed through the gateway which connects the Gardens of Ialou with the world known to the living. It is a magnificent monumental gate framed with two maple trees of precious jewels as brilliant as the dawn.

The magic ship which carried the lord Ra was provided with a complete crew like any of the ships which sailed the Nile. It had a pilot in the prow to sound the depths and determine the wind, and another pilot at the helm to steer; between them, in the middle of the boat, was a sailor to pass the word aft, as well as the other sailors who manned the ship. More than once, Apep the huge serpent appeared, surging out of the water in the path of the god Ra, and barring his passage; and at that very moment men saw the sun darken and disappear.

Then the crew summoned up their courage and began to pray: the monster must be frightened away by noise, by loud cries, by music. They beat sharply on any metal object they could find. They leaped about, clapped their hands, beat their breasts. What an agonising suspense!

They went on until the noise and clamour, mounting up to the skies, made the monster take fright. At last, the sun, restored to life, came out of the shadows and took up its radiant course once again, while Apep retreated into the depths, paralysed by the magic of the gods and pierced with twenty wounds. Now when this happens we speak of it as an eclipse of the sun.

During the time when Ra lived on earth, in his castle at Heliopolis, he was in the habit of embarking each day to make his customary journey around the earth, returning twelve hours later. Each province in turn saw him arrive and in each of them he remained a whole hour to settle affairs of state. He held audience for everyone, however humble or however important, and he listened to their problems, settled their quarrels, acted as judge at their trials. To every deserving person he gave a plot of land from the royal estates which became his property, and each family received sufficient money for its own maintenance. He sympathised with the people's suffering and did his best to alleviate it. He taught everyone the most effective means of protecting themselves against reptiles, and he gave them the magic words for frightening away serpents and fierce animals, the charms for driving off evil spirits, and the best remedies for illness.

He gave away so much that he himself was left with only one talisman: the name which his mother and father had given him at birth, and which they divulged to no one but himself. This he held hidden in his heart for fear that a sorcerer might discover it and use it to make his spells more effective; for the only way by which real harm can be done to a living being is by discovering his secret name, which it is forbidden to utter.

Nevertheless, like all living things, the lord Ra began to grow old. Magnificent and powerful in middle life, he began to decline; his body shrank and became bent, he was forced to lean on a stick to support his weakened frame.

He became infirm; his limbs began to shake and saliva dropped to the ground from his trembling mouth.

Then Isis conceived the idea of robbing him of his secret so that she might own the world and make herself a goddess, by using the sacred name so well hidden and so powerful. Isis, until that time one of Pharaoh's humble servants, was shallow and skilful with words, and had a heart more cunning than a million men, more malicious than a million gods and spirits. Just like Ra, nothing was unknown to her in the heavens or on the earth except this mysterious name of invincible power.

Violence was no use at all. Although Ra was well advanced in years, he was still a god. No one in the world was strong enough to fight against him.

So Isis thought up the most ingenious of stratagems. In those days, whenever a man or a woman fell ill, the only chance of a cure was by finding out their secret name and, by this name, exorcising the evil spirit that was believed to be the cause of the malady. Isis, therefore, decided to infect Ra with a terrible illness so that she might offer to look after him and save his life. While looking after him she plotted to force him to surrender this hidden word, this secret and indispensable name.

She thought that his suffering would induce him to divulge it in order that she might use it to exorcise the demon and rid his body of the sickness.

She gathered up some mud on to which the divine

saliva had fallen and then moulded it with her skilful hands. She gave it the form of a sacred serpent, then she buried it in the dust of the road and brought it to life by reciting the magic formula which can animate all inanimate things.

Passing this spot one morning on his usual daily journey, Ra was bitten in the heel. The god uttered a cry of pain, his frightened voice reaching up into the skies. Not knowing what kind of sting was forcing itself into his flesh, he called out, "What is it, what is it?" and all the gods answered, "What can it be?"

Ra could not reply. He was choking with rage and pain, his lips were trembling, all his limbs jerked convulsively, while the venom spread through his flesh, taking possession of his whole being, just as the Nile swallows up the land in times of flood.

Recovering a little, Ra stammered out, "I—I have been st . . stung by something which has entered into me and given me terrible pain. My heart felt it and still feels it although my eyes can see nothing. My hand did not create it, it does not resemble any of the creatures I have made. Assuredly, no one has ever suffered so much, nor endured such pain!

"This is worse than any known agony. It is not fire, and yet my heart feels devoured by flames; it is not water, yet my body trembles and all my limbs are shaking.

"Bring me the children of the gods that they may pronounce the magic words which will charm away the demons."

Then came the children of the gods, each with his books of spells, his recipes, his formulae and his store of wisdom. Isis herself came forward complacently with her sorcery and her spells to stop the pain which was racking the patient. Her mouth was filled with the breath of life, her words gave life to the breathless, and revived the dying.

She said: "What is it? What ails you, O father of the gods? What creature has stung you? What sting has pierced your hallowed flesh? Is it a serpent which has caused you this suffering? Has one of your children risen up against you? Assuredly, with the right incantation it is possible to kill this enemy. He will be forced to retreat in the face of your radiance."

Ra learned from Isis the cause of his torment. He was astonished and began to complain more than ever.

"So it is that while leaving for my daily journey across the land of Egypt and over my mountains, in order to cast my eyes over all that I have created, I was stung by a serpent lying in the dust which I did not even see.

"It is not water, and yet I shiver far more than if I had been soaked. It is not fire and yet I burn more fiercely than if I were in the middle of a blazing furnace. All my limbs are streaming with sweat, I shudder, my eyes flicker and I can no longer see the sky. My face is dripping with water as on a day of exceptional heat in a humid summer."

Isis obligingly offered to help him and suggested that she should try to cure him with the aid of a magic remedy, an infallible incantation which had only to be uttered to cast out the most dangerous and tenacious ailment. Then she discreetly explained that this remedy was only effective if the secret name of the sick person were introduced into the incantation. "Tell me your name, O divine father, for you know that these charms do not work unless the secret name is used."

At the first hint of this, Ra, suspicious and vaguely sensing a trap, tried to evade the issue and then to deceive Isis. He calmly enumerated all his titles, all the names he had been given, one after the other. He called upon the universe to witness that he used his real name—Khepri—in the morning, Ra at midday, Toumu in the evening and then Atouni.

"I have," said he, "many names and many forms. I am he who created heaven and earth and who placed there the souls of the gods. I am he who, on opening his eyes, brings light into the world."

Isis, the crafty one, insisted. And she succeeded in obtaining his assurance that his secret name was no illusion, that it really did exist. Ra declared: "My father and my mother gave me my secret name and they told me what it was. It has been hidden in my body since the day of my birth, so that the power of its magic may not pass into the hands of some sorceress, who might wish to use it against me."

And, to deceive Isis, he went on to talk about other things and to enumerate once again all the names he had been given. "I am he who created heaven and earth and who gave souls to the gods. I am he who, on opening his eyes, brings forth light and, on closing them, brings darkness to the world; he also who orders the Nile to let its waters flow, and of whose name the gods themselves are ignorant. I am Khepri in the morning and at noon I am Ra. I have still more names: I am Harma Khouiti, the summer sun and the noon sun; I am also Atoumu, the autumn sun and the setting sun."

Isis was not deceived, but she did not waver. She began by reciting a series of magic words which are all-powerful, calling the invalid by the name of Khepri; but the illness did not loosen its grip. Then she recited the same words, giving the invalid the name of Ra. Finally she spoke the charm again, calling him Atoumu. And still there was no result. She waited to see what would happen without saying a word.

And all the time the venom from the sacred saliva spread through the body of the god Ra which continued to burn even though it was paralysed. The sufferings, far from becoming less, were becoming more acute.

Then Isis said to Ra: "None of the names you gave me is your real name, your secret name. Confess it, tell it to me, and immediately, in the time it takes to repeat the formula, you will be cured. For this spell cannot work unless the patient is called by his real name."

Ra, consumed by a raging fire, burnt as though flames were licking his body, was finally beaten by this intolerable pain. He pronounced the fateful words: "I allow myself to be persuaded by Isis. My name shall pass from my body into her body. I consent that you shall carve me open, O mother Isis, so that my name may pass from my heart to yours."

Isis did what was necessary, for the secret name was hidden in the body, and in order to reveal it the chest had to be opened up, just as the corpse is opened up for embalming when it is turned into a mummy.

So the god hid himself from the other gods and, when the moment arrived for Ra to give up his secret, Isis learned his true name. Then very swiftly she pronounced the incantation, using the secret name of Ra, and the venom was drawn out. The illness, put to flight by the spell, disappeared, the poison ceased to torment Ra whose pain was suddenly relieved and forgotten.

But Isis, by virtue of the name which Ra had delivered to her with his heart, now held the secret of his power. She lost no time in making herself a goddess.

In this way, a woman's wiles had despoiled the great god Ra of his last secret, of his last talisman.

Meanwhile, old age had overcome Ra little by little and soon he was so much altered that the day came when men themselves, in spite of the dazzling effect that Ra in all his glory had upon them, realised how decrepit he had become.

Then they began to talk about it between themselves: ". . . see how His Majesty is growing old; his bones are silver, his flesh is golden, his hair is lapis lazuli . . ." and much unfriendly gossip which showed a lowering of the respect due to a god.

The lord Ra heard the gossip being talked about him by the human beings and he gave orders to the men of his suite: "Bring before me my divine Nile; Shu and Tefnut; Sibou as well, and Nut; all the gods, the fathers and mothers who were with me when I was in the void in the chaos of the beginning of things. Chaos itself. Let each of the gods bring with him his own circle of gods. Bring them before me in secret, to the great castle so that they may listen to my problems and give me their advice."

The council of the gods, which was like a family council, met in the presence of the ancestors of Ra and also of his future descendants who were floating in the waters of the beginning of time waiting to be born: his

children Shu and Tefnut, his grandchildren Sibou and
Nut, they were all there.

They arranged themselves in a circle around the throne
of Ra. Following the custom, they prostrated themselves
in the dust before his majesty, the forehead touching the
ground, and then the meeting began. Ra pronounced the
following words:

"O you, the most ancient of gods and my elder from
whom I had my being, and you, O ancestral gods, see
how the men of my own creation intend to rise up against
me! They resent my majesty. Tell me what you think,
for I have called you together to learn what you would
say to my proposals, before I put them all to death—as I
intend to do."

Nou, the most ancient of them all, was the first to speak
and he asked that a proper trial be held so that the
culprits could be sentenced in a lawful manner and those
responsible could be proved guilty.

"My son Ra, a god even greater than the god who
made you, more ancient than the gods who created you,
administers justice in the place which is yours, and the
terror will be great indeed when your gaze lights upon
those who plot against you."

Ra observed that if royal justice were carried out in its
full solemnity, men warned of what would happen to
them would not wait to put in an appearance before the
throne of Ra, but would escape into the desert, where
they would be safe from arrest. For the guardian gods of
Egypt could not pursue them into the desert. It was the
inviolable refuge.

The council of the gods, convinced that the fears of Ra
were justified, decided that man should be massacred

without prior judgment. The divine eye would be the executioner.

"Make use of your eye, Ra, to deal with those who have plotted to overthrow you, for there is no eye as mighty as yours when it assumes the form of Sekhmet."

And thus it was done. The eye of Ra took the form of the goddess Sekhmet and swooped down without any warning upon men, following them over mountain and valley, with great sweeps of a knife.

At the end of several hours, the god Ra, who did not really want to destroy the human race and was tired of the bloodshed, ordered the massacre to cease.

But the goddess had tasted blood and she refused to obey.

"Upon thy life," replied the goddess, "when I murder men my heart rejoices," and, as she acknowledged her oath on the life of Ra, she touched her nose and her ear and put her hands on her head. This is why the Egyptians called her Sekhmet the mighty, the lioness, the wild beast, she who struck and overcame without pity; this is also why she is represented with the head of a lion on the body of a woman. Intoxicated with blood, Sekhmet would not stop killing.

Nightfall alone put a stop to her journey over the houses and streets of Heliopolis, where for hours she had unceasingly trampled in the blood.

Ra profited by the darkness of the night to lay a trap for her and put an end to her rage. He said, "Let messengers be brought before me who are skilful and swift, who can fly like the wind." These messengers were immediately brought to him.

Then his majesty said: "Let them run to Elephantine

and bring me back mandrakes of special quality and a
heap of huge pomegranates."

As soon as they had brought back a quantity of mandrakes and a heap of pomegranates, the god sent for the
miller of Heliopolis so that he could grind them up.
Meanwhile, the servants had crushed grain to make beer
and prepared it ready to brew. They mixed the crushed
mandrakes and the juice of the pressed pomegranates with
the beer and the blood of men. Seven thousand pitchers
were filled with this mixture. Ra himself tasted the en-
ticing beverage and carefully verified the virtues of the
potion.

"It is good," he said, "with this brew, I will save men
from the fury of the goddess. Fill your arms with these
pitchers and take them to the place where she has
massacred so many men."

Then the great master made the dawn appear in the
middle of the night so that they could see clearly to pour
out on to the earth the liquid which filled the seven
thousand jugs. The earth drank it up and the fields were
flooded far and wide, and the sheet of liquid reached at
least as high as four tall palm trees.

The goddess awoke in the morning ready to begin the
slaughter again, but she found everywhere flooded and
her face softened at the sight. She was thirsty and she
drank. When she had quenched her thirst with the liquid
which, thanks to the strange mixture gave the illusion of
the blood of men, her heart was softened. She went off
replete, intoxicated and satisfied and thought no more
about killing men.

But Ra, in his wisdom which foresaw the future,
thought that later on, when she became sober again, she

would be capable of returning to her former state of fury. Therefore he initiated certain rites so that this evil might be avoided, and that at one and the same time he might tell future generations of the punishment he had inflicted on the impious, and also compensate Sekhmet for the loss of her victims. He decided, therefore, that every day of the year there should be brewed as many jugs of beer as there were priestesses of the sun, and then afterwards men would make jugs of beer to offer the goddess on her birthday. As for the date of the massacre, men have never forgotten it. That is why the fifth of the month of Tybi is a hostile day, a very unfriendly day.

Time passed, and the day came when Ra, tired and old, began to think of rest.

"By my life," he said to his circle of gods (and he did not forget to touch his nose and ear, nor to place his two hands on his head), "my heart is too weary to remain any longer among men. In any case, I should soon be once more obliged to begin all over again to do away with them to the last man. The gift of death is not the one I like to make."

The gods, surprised, cried out in reply: "Do not speak of weariness at a time when you have just been triumphant. It would be better not to utter a word."

But Ra did not listen to them. He had decided to abandon this realm where his creatures dared to whisper against him, and he addressed himself to Nou. "My limbs are decrepit and for the first time I am overcome with weakness. I want to hide the humiliation of old age. I want to go from hence, but I want to go to a place where no one can reach me."

So an inaccessible place had to be found for him, and

that was difficult to find in a universe still badly organised and imperfect. Nou ordained that Shu, the son of Ra, should occupy the throne of his father and govern men with the energy of a young god. And to give Ra refuge where nothing could reach him, he decided to complete his work and to finish off the creation of the world.

Nou in his majesty declared: "Son Shu, you are to act for your father, Ra. You must accomplish his will. And you, Nut, my daughter, take your father Ra upon your back and hold him suspended above the earth."

Nut replied: "And how shall I do that, O Nou, my father?" But she obeyed meekly. She changed herself into a cow, and placed His Majesty King Ra upon her back.

But when the men who had survived the massacre came to do homage to the lord Ra, who had saved them and protected them against the knife of Sekhmet, he was no longer there in his palace. An enormous cow, certainly celestial in origin, was standing there, and they could make out Ra on the cow's back. He had such an air of being determined to leave the earth that they did not even dare to try to dissuade him. Nevertheless, they wished to give him proof of their repentance and also to be worthy of his forgiveness, and so they said to him: "Wait until tomorrow, O Ra, our master, and we will overthrow before your eyes those of your enemies who have threatened you and plotted against you."

So His Majesty Ra came down from the cow's back and returned to his palace. At that moment the earth was plunged into darkness.

But when the earth lighted up with the new day, men came out with their bows and arrows and began to direct their missiles against the enemies of Ra and to vanquish them in front of him.

Whereupon Ra said to them, "Your sins are forgiven, for the sacrifice of the guilty redeems the faults of other men."

From that day dates the blood sacrifice. Every time men offended the god—and this often happened—it was understood that to wipe out the fault, they must sacrifice the guilty so as to appease the divine anger and obtain forgiveness for all. And the memory of the anger of Ra and of the destructive fury of Sekhmet made men hasten to punish the guilty so that the vengeance due to them should not fall on all men.

Nevertheless, the heart of Ra was tender towards men, his creatures! It was repugnant to him to see them sacrifice each other, even though guilty. He decreed, therefore, that animals should be sacrificed in their place and that oxen, gazelles and birds would be acceptable victims for the gods, on condition that the sacrificial priest did not forget to pronounce the magic words which made their sacrifice take the place of men.

Having concluded this contract of alliance which reconciled him with the surviving men, the great Ra returned to the celestial cow and climbed on to its back. Then Nut arose and braced her four legs like a vault, but still she sagged under the load. She begged to be upheld, feeling her strength leaving her and her legs weakening.

Then Ra said, "My son Shu, put yourself under my daughter to support her until she can bear me. Hold her with that pillar over there and these here in the shadow; hold her above your head and be her shepherd."

Shu obeyed and Nut was succoured. Her stomach,

stretched out like a ceiling, was well supported and held up by four columns, which were watched over by Horus the Hawk to the south, by Sat to the north, by Thoth to the west and by Sapdi to the east. It was the celestial vault, and the universe was at last furnished with a sky, where Ra, the all-powerful god, set about organising the greatly enlarged new world which he discovered upon the back of the cow. He established his residence there in two different places, in the Field of Plants to begin with and then in the Field of Rest. He dwells there in the heavens, far from the earth and from men.

2

Isis and Osiris

Osiris

NE day, Nut, the goddess of heaven, and Sibou, god of the earth, had married without the knowledge of Ra, who would not have given his permission. He was exceedingly angry when he was told about their wedding. He cast a powerful spell upon Nut so that she should never be able to bear children in any month of the year. He thought thus to punish her for marrying Sibou without his consent. Nut was in despair. What was the use of being married unless she could have children?

But the god Thoth had pity on her in her grief. He played a game of draughts with the moon and he was the winner. They played again and again he won. After several games, as he was always the winner, he could ask what he liked of the moon. So he asked for and was given a seventy-second part of her fire and her light—enough to create five whole days.

Now, these five days did not belong to any month. They were outside the normal year and not within the calendar, so that during that time Nut was able to escape the prohibition of Ra, and bring several children into the world. She managed to have five children one after the other. On the first of these five days won from the moon, it was Osiris who was born at Thebes. He was handsome, with a smooth dark skin, and he was tall; more than fifteen feet in height. At the time of his birth a mysterious voice announced—"The Master of all things has seen the light of day". Cries of joy spread throughout the earth, but soon they turned to tears and wailing, for the voice went on to foretell that terrible sufferings would afflict the newly-born. A certain man named Pampyles of Thebes, who was going to fetch water from the temple, heard—he was the only person to hear it this time—the voice which commanded him to proclaim that Osiris, the great king, the benefactor of the world, had just been born. He obeyed the command, and so the gods entrusted him with feeding the child and bringing him up in preparation for a very special destiny. As for Ra, in his faraway dwelling, he heard the echo and the tumult of the announcement, and his heart rejoiced because he had long ago forgiven Nut. His great-grandson came to live with him, and he had him brought up as befitted the heir to the throne.

The second day it was Harveris who was born, and the third day it was Set. The fourth day it was Isis, and finally, on the last day, it was Nephtys. These were all the children of Nut, and the great-grandchildren of Ra.

Osiris grew ever taller. Later he married Isis his sister. When he became king, she was of great help to him in all his undertakings.

In those days, the Egyptians were half savage. They ate each other and lived by the fruits of the earth, but they could not do anything for themselves. They were barely capable of defending themselves against wild beasts.

Osiris taught them to recognise the plants which were suitable to eat—corn, barley and grapes, which until that time grew side by side with weeds and grass. He taught them how to make a plough and a hoe with which to till the land, and he made them turn over the soil in the fields and drain away the flood of water; he showed them how to sow and how to reap the corn and the barley, and how to prune the vines. Before their astonished eyes, Osiris pressed the juice from the grapes and drank the first draught of wine! And, since all the land was not suitable for grapes, he taught them how to make a fermented drink from barley, which was, of course, beer.

Isis in her turn explained to them that they ought not to eat each other. She looked after them, and healed their sickness by giving them good remedies, and by sending away the evil spirits who were the cause of their troubles. She also taught them to live together in a house, husband and wife with their children. She showed them how to cut the ears of corn and grind the grain between two flat stones, how to knead the flour into dough, and how to bake bread. She spun thread with the stalks of flax; she also invented the method of weaving. Her sister, Nephtys, seated before her, stretched the thread, threw the shuttle and wove the cloth; then the two of them bleached it.

Men did not know that the earth itself held riches for

them. Osiris taught them to recognise the metals in their seams, he made them work gold and forge brass. From that time onwards they knew how to make weapons for killing wild beasts, tools to work with, and, later, statues to represent the gods.

For Osiris had also taught them to respect the gods and to worship them. He fixed the exact offering due to each of them; he arranged the order of ceremony, the words which were to be pronounced, the tone and the rhythm of the chants. He had the most beautiful temples erected, and sought to reproduce the image of the gods. Finally, he built whole towns, and probably rebuilt Thebes, the city in which he was born.

He did even more than this for men. With Thoth the Ibis, the animal with paws and tail the colour of lapis lazuli and a body the colour of jade, and with the help of Thoth the Baboon, the god who knows how to measure time, count the days, number the months and calculate the years, Osiris undertook to give to men the learning of the gods, who understood all things seen and unseen.

Thoth, the lord of the voice, the master of speech and of lions, taught them to understand the signs he had invented to represent words, which would preserve better than the memory the phrases and the formulae obeyed by the whole world. Then men knew that wonderful thing—how to write. And those who were the followers and disciples of Thoth were all wise men and soothsayers, skilful scribes, whose precious manuscripts contained the divine wisdom. And Thoth and Osiris taught them to look at the course of the stars in the sky, and gave them also the knowledge of a life beyond the earthly one.

Having proved himself a model king, just and peace-loving, Osiris desired now to be a great conqueror and tamer of peoples. He entrusted to Queen Isis the government of Egypt during his absence and, gathering together a great army, he set off to cross the whole of Asia, with Thoth the Ibis and Anubis the Jackal.

However, he was a conqueror who never employed force and violence and murderous weapons. He conquered by gentleness and persuasion. Songs, in which the human voice was accompanied by the sound of musical instruments, softened the hearts of men, and they were persuaded to learn all the things he had taught the Egyptians. So they called him the Good-one, Ounnefer, one who devotes himself to man's well-being. No land escaped his mission and he returned to the banks of the Nile, having travelled the world and spread civilisation from one horizon to the other. He came back in a boat whose crew each had one oar of cypress and one of juniper.

But he was doomed to perish by ingratitude and the force of evil.

Nearby lived his brother, the impious and violent Set Typhon, who typified the evil which exists alongside the good. He was the third son of Nut, white of skin and red of hair, red as a donkey with a red mane (that is why donkeys are sacred to him). He was a violent character, jealous and gloomy as well as wicked. In the absence of his brother, Osiris, he wanted to be the king and the master of all Egypt and it was only with great difficulty that Isis was able to prevent his plotting.

On the return of Osiris, there was great rejoicing in Memphis to welcome the traveller whom they delighted in calling the Lord of the Green Fields, the Master of the Blossoming Vines and the God of the Cornfields.

Set took advantage of this occasion to seize the throne. Like a good brother, he invited Osiris to a great banquet which was prepared in his honour, attended by seventy-two trusted officers who were the evil one's accomplices.

Secretly he had measured the exact height of Osiris, and had had specially made a chest of rare wood of the same length and very curiously wrought. He commanded that this casket should be brought during the banquet into the hall where the guests were assembled. Everyone cried out in admiration at the beauty of the chest. As they all seemed to covet this masterpiece, Set began to laugh and to say jokingly that he would willingly make a gift of it to anyone whom it exactly fitted. Immediately, one after another tried to stretch his form into the chest, but there was always a big space left.

Osiris tried in his turn. Immediately the officers surrounded the casket. The lid was snapped down and solidly locked and molten lead was used to secure it even more firmly. Then, in a flash, it was lifted up and carried away by the conspirators and launched on to the Nile, where the current swept it rapidly out to sea.

The news of this terrible crime spread terror among gods and men. Swiftly the gods who were friends of Osiris hid themselves in the bodies of animals to escape the wrath of Set, who doubtless would make them suffer like his brother if he could lay his hands on them. Isis became deeply distressed; she tore her garments, cut her long hair as a sign of mourning, and set off in search of the chest. She hastened to every corner of the land, eaten up with anxiety and making enquiries of all whom she met.

She searched for a long time without respite, for this was the Quest of Isis. She travelled around the world lamenting, determined not to stop until she had found the object for which she sought.

Thoth, Osiris and Isis

THE QUEST OF ISIS

S soon as the crime was accomplished, the assassin, Set, the wicked god, took the precaution of shutting Isis up in a room in his house, so that she could not go in search of the corpse which, with the help of his confederates, he had flung into the Nile.

But Isis managed to escape from her prison.

She met Thoth, the great god, the prince of truth, who said to her: "Come, O goddess Isis, have courage and confide in me, I will guide and help you. Hide yourself away, and it will come to pass that you will have a son. He will become tall and he will be as handsome as he is strong. He will sit upon his father's throne, will avenge him, and will become the king of the two crowns, the most powerful of all the monarchs to rule over the whole world."

But the goddess, Isis, at that moment was not thinking about the little Horus who was not yet born. She was thinking only of recovering the body of her murdered husband so that she might lay it in the tomb.

She succeeded then in leaving the house of Set during the night. Thanks to Thoth, she was escorted by seven scorpions, which were charged with stinging anyone who threatened her or even tried to come near her. Two of them went on ahead, to make sure that the road was clear, two others went beside her, one to the right and the other to the left, thus protecting her on both sides. The three remaining scorpions brought up the rear a little distance behind. They had all been given very exacting and strict orders from Thoth that they were not to speak to anyone; they must go straight ahead, their eyes fixed on the ground, examining the route, for all serpents and vipers were in the service of Set.

The two who went ahead, Tefen and Befen, led Isis as far as the town of Pa-Sin, at the beginning of the papyrus marshes. As they entered into the town, through which they had to pass, the women who were seated spinning on their doorsteps were most curious about the strange procession. One of them, fearing that she would be asked to give shelter to Isis who was dragging herself along so painfully, tired out with the long journey, went into her home and slammed the door loudly in the face of the goddess, because she was so terrified at the sight of this escort of scorpions. At this insult, the seven protectors stopped to confer. After some discussion, six of them, one after another, approached their leader and injected their venom into his tail.

Meanwhile, a peasant who lived a little further on and was called Taha, left her own threshold to come forward and welcome the unknown traveller, whom she never suspected was the goddess Isis. She invited her to come and rest in her house, and Isis went into the little hovel of this poor but hospitable woman.

The leader of the scorpions, with its tail filled with poison, slipped under the door of the house belonging to the unwelcoming woman, Usa, the one who had so rudely slammed the door in the face of the goddess, and stung her little child. Immediately, as if by magic, the house caught fire and began to burn fiercely and there was no water to be found anywhere to quench the flames.

The heart of Usa was filled with anguish for she thought that her son was going to die as no one could live long after being stung by a large scorpion. Then she ran through the streets of the town calling for help, but no one answered her appeal, no one dared to leave the house.

It was Isis herself who came to her aid. The goddess had pity on the little child and she wished with all her heart that the innocent creature might be saved.

She cried out, calling the woman, Usa: "Come and find me! Come and find me! My mouth holds the breath of life. My powers are famed in my own country. My father taught me the secret of casting out the demon of death. I, his well-beloved daughter, I have this power!"

Then Isis stretched out her hands over the child in its mother's arms and repeated this spell: "O poison of Tefen, come forth out of the body of this child, fall down on to the earth and penetrate no further into the infant's flesh. O poison of Tefen, come out, fall down on to the earth! I am Isis the goddess, mistress of magic words and potent spells. I know how to compile formulae which will cure; I know how to pronounce words which charm away illness! Give ear to my words. Let each of you reptiles who have stung the child see his poison falling to the earth. Obey my voice! I am speaking, O Scorpions! I am alone and in anguish. I wish that the child should live and that the poison should no longer affect him. In the name of Ra, the living god, let the power of the venom weaken. Let Horus be saved by his mother, Isis, and let him who has been stung also be saved."

Then suddenly, although it was not the rainy season, water fell from the cloudless skies and put out the flames of the burning house and everything was restored to its former state. The fury of the heavens was conquered by the intervention of Isis. The woman, Usa, greatly distressed at having shut her door in the face of Isis, brought gifts for the goddess and was deeply sorry for not having recognised her. The little child's life was saved, thanks to the incantation of Isis, and when his mother saw him recovered and full of joy, she went back a second time to her neighbour's house carrying many good things for the goddess.

Soon Isis went on her way in search of her husband's body.

However, the evil spirits of the road, the servants of Set, went before her and spread panic, so that men were seized with terror and hid themselves so well that Isis did not meet a single person of whom she could make enquiries.

One day, however, she saw some little children playing by the roadside and she asked them: "Little children, have you seen some men go by here carrying a long heavy chest?"

"Yes," they replied. "We have seen them, and they threw the chest into that branch of the Nile which passes through Tanis, but the current must long ago have carried it out to sea."

"Truly," lamented Isis, trembling with sorrow. "Let this branch of the Nile be accursed and twice accursed! But you, my little children, whenever by chance you let words fall from your lips when you are playing on the steps of the temple, the wise men will pay attention to them, and in days to come your childish sayings will be taken as warnings and prophecies, because you have given the questing Isis precious information."

Then she continued her journey, still accompanied by the faithful scorpions. She followed the trails of sweet clover which bordered the roads, for she knew that wherever Osiris had passed, the little flowers would spring up, so she followed his trail with the help of the scent and the blooms. She pressed on and on and on, for the coffin containing the remains of Osiris had been carried by the waves of the sea as far as Byblos in Syria, the town of Adonis. The chest had run aground on the shore, and a bush hid it from view.

Through the power of the celestial corpse, this bush became an enormous acacia tree, so tall, so beautiful and so thick that its trunk grew around the chest, enveloping it and completely hiding it from view. In due course, Malcandre, the king of the country, discovered this magnificent tree, and had it cut down. Without suspecting the existence of the coffin, he had it fashioned into one of the pillars to support the roof of his palace.

Soon after this the unfortunate Isis, still seeking her husband's body, eventually reached Byblos. Tired and suffering, she sat down near a fountain and would not speak to anyone. She awaited the night to change herself

into a swallow and it was thus that she discovered the
trunk of the acacia used as a pillar in the king's palace and
still containing the coffin of Osiris. Every night she flew
round the pillar, uttering cries of distress, but no one
paid any attention. At last, Isis decided to take action.
One day, when the servants of the Queen passed by the
fountain, they saw this woman, silent and suffering as
usual. But on this particular day she greeted them and
entered into conversation with them. This was easy, for
there was nothing the Queen's servants liked better than
to gossip.

The stranger offered to dress their hair and arrange it
in the fashion of her country. She let them smell the
delicate perfume with which her own hair was scented,
and she offered to procure some for them. Naturally,
they allowed themselves to be adorned, and to have their
hair dressed and scented according to the custom of the
stranger's far-away country. But when they returned to
the palace, the Queen soon detected this perfume of the
gods. When she was told where it came from, she asked
to see the stranger immediately. Isis was sent for and the
Queen was captivated by her pleasing ways.

She kept the goddess near her like a friend and even
entrusted her with the care of her little child. Of course,
she was unaware of all the strange ways of this new nurse.
She did not know, for instance, that to feed the baby, Isis
simply placed a thumb in its mouth! Neither did she
know that every night, Isis changed herself into a swallow
and flew around the great column of the palace looking
for a means of taking possession of it and its contents.

However, it happened one night that the Queen, feeling anxious, arose from her bed and went to see what was

happening in her little child's room. What a surprise awaited her! The infant was sleeping peacefully, but he was surrounded by high flames which burnt without smoke, whilst seven huge scorpions were carefully guarding him!

On hearing the Queen's cries, the King, the servants and even Isis herself, came running to the room. With a gesture, Isis quickly put out the flames, and the scorpions disappeared. "You did not put your trust in me," she said. "Your son will never be immortal. Every night, I put him into the flames to purge him of his earthly characteristics. It is all over now. I can do no more for him."

Then the Queen was extremely sad and the King, honoured at having sheltered a goddess beneath his roof, asked what he could do to show his gratitude. Isis implored him to give her the great pillar. Immediately the King had the carpenters brought before him, and they, with a few strokes of their axes, quickly felled the acacia. Isis herself split open the trunk. When she had pulled out Osiris' coffin, she scented the trunk which had held it with a precious essence, wrapped it in fine linen and gave it to the King and Queen and the people of Byblos, to whom it became an object of veneration.

Then Isis, the goddess, went on her way, taking with her the coffin which held the body of Osiris, her brother and her husband. The King sent his two eldest sons to accompany her and to do her honour. Hardly had she started, however, than Isis stopped the procession, and had the coffin opened so that she might look on the dead face of her husband. At the sight of him, her cries of anguish and her trembling filled the air with such horror that the younger son of the King became mad for the rest of his life.

Meanwhile, Isis, leaning over the open coffin, had put her head against the face of Osiris and was weeping. Suddenly, lifting up her eyes she saw that the eldest son of the King was looking at her curiously. Furious at being thus spied upon, she threw him a terrible glance, so that, seized with uncontrollable terror, he fell dead to the ground.

Without troubling herself any more about the fate of the princes of Byblos, Isis continued on her way. After many difficulties, she brought back the coffin and the remains of Osiris to Egypt. She laid them to rest near Buto, in a lonely and secluded place where no one ever ventured.

THE MOURNING OF ISIS AND THE RESURRECTION OF OSIRIS

VENTUALLY, Isis settled down in Buto, the town where she was born, in the middle of the marshes of reeds and bulrushes which protected her against the violence of Typhon. More than once since her time, these same marshes and these same bulrushes have served to protect even Pharaoh himself against the attacks of enemies.

It was in this peace that Isis brought into the world her son, the young Horus; it was there among the rushes that she fed him, and there he grew tall; it was there that she brought him up in secret, far from the wiles of the evil one.

Nevertheless, the evil Set, hunting in the moonlight, saw the coffin in the secluded spot where Isis had hidden it. He opened it and recognised the corpse of Osiris. Immediately, he saw his chance to destroy the evidence of his foul deed by tearing the remains of his brother to pieces. So he cut up the corpse into fourteen pieces which he flung in every direction. The unfortunate Isis no sooner learnt of this second crime than she again took up her sad pilgrimage, this time in search of the shreds of her husband's body. One by one, she succeeded in finding them with the exception of a single fragment which had dropped into the water and had been devoured by the serpent, who greedily swallowed up anything that was thrown into the Nile.

Each time that the goddess found one of the sad fragments of the body, she raised up a tomb on the exact spot, and led the priests in charge of the fourteen sanctuaries to believe that each of them possessed the whole body of Osiris. In course of time, these sanctuaries became known as the stages of the sorrowful voyage called the "Quest of Isis".

When she had collected together all these pitiful pieces, the goddess Isis called in the help of Nephthys, her sister, Horus, her beloved son, Thoth the Ibis and Anubis the Jackal. Together these companions, the heirs of the learning of Osiris and the recipients of his thoughts, discovered, in the teachings of the god himself, the means of bringing him back to new life. By the same means, Isis discovered the "remedy which gives immortality". With Nephthys and Horus and Thoth and Anubis, she put together the fragments of the body of Osiris and embalmed them. She then made them into an imperishable mummy able to keep for all eternity the soul of this god. This was the very first mummy.

Anubis the Jackal had for a long time understood the mysterious science which could ensure the preservation of human flesh; but he had succeeded in obtaining only one dried body, stiff and frozen which could not rise up nor stir and which was condemned to lead a gloomy existence among the shadows. Thoth and Isis and Horus were anxious that Osiris should be more favoured than this, so they included in the preparation of the mummy some magic rites which would obtain a new existence for the dried flesh. This is how they set about it.

Each time Isis had found a piece of the body she had breathed new life into it. She then enclosed all the pieces in a figure made of wax, aromatic herbs, earth mixed with grain, incense and precious stones. The figure was the same size as Osiris, and made in his image. Then she carried out some magic on this figure. And Isis and Nephthys said to it: "You have regained your head, you have brought together your flesh; you have been given back your veins: your limbs have been re-assembled."

Then Sibou, the father of Osiris, presided over the ceremony, and Ra from the sky sent the goddesses Vautour and Urus, those who encircled as with a crown the foreheads of the gods, to set the head of Osiris firmly on his neck. The statue was enveloped in a carefully arranged linen shroud and Isis and Nephthys, dressed in mourning, their hair dishevelled, beating their breasts, began to wail in lamentation, beseeching Osiris to come back and inhabit his reconstructed form.

Isis chanted as she kissed the feet of the mummy: "Come to your own dwelling; your enemies are no longer here. Come to your house! Look at me; it is I, your sister whom you love. Do not keep away from me. Come back to your house now! When I do not see you, my heart grieves for you. My eyes seek you; I run in every direction to find you. Come to the one who loves you. Ounnefer, come to your sister, come to your wife. O you whose heart no longer beats, come back to your dwelling; do not stay away from me; gods and men both weep for you; and I, I call you, crying up to the sky . . . Do you not hear my voice? It is I, whom you loved on earth, and you love nobody more than me."

Nephthys, leaning on the head of the mummy, said in her turn: "O handsome prince, come back to your dwelling to rejoice my heart. None of your enemies is here. It is your two sisters who stay beside you, guarding your funeral litter and they call you, weeping: come back to them, come and see them . . . your enemies are overcome. See I am with you to protect your limbs. Come back to us, our prince, our lord. Do not remain far from us."

Then they wrapped the mummy in another shroud of fine linen which they fixed with narrow bands, according to custom. They inscribed the bands with sacred figures and magic formulae; they arranged on the limbs amulets which bore powerful charms. They carved also on the sides of the coffin and on the walls of the mortuary-chamber scenes of the earthly life and of the life beyond the tomb, and sang incantations to bring back to Osiris the use of his eyes to see, of his ears to hear, of his mouth to eat and speak, of his hands to act, of his legs to walk. These formulae they inscribed in *The Book of the Opening of the Mouth*.

They did even more than this. They set up beside the coffin which contained the mummy, a statue in the image of Osiris, and they put it in the charge of dressers, with instructions to carry out a detailed toilet of washings, fumigations and anointings. Then they clothed the statue with bands of green, red, yellow and white. Afterwards, they fashioned in cornelian, in precious stones and in gold, the swastika, the sign of life, the necklets, the bracelets and the anklets which were designed to ward off Set-the-adversary-and-the-enemy and render him powerless. To the statue also they chanted their magic songs to open his mouth, his eyes and his ears, to bring life to his arms and his legs, to give breath to his throat, and to rouse up the beating of his heart.

The formulae which they repeated were so powerful that the counterpart, this statue in the image of Osiris, lived and heard, spoke and ate, seated before a table filled with all sorts of good things, which the sky gives and the earth creates and the Nile brings out of its depths. And the bread, the meat, the fruit and the potions kept him for ever free from hunger and thirst.

Thus revitalised, Osiris could have taken again his place among men, and sometimes it did happen that he revealed himself to his faithful servants, but he did not wish to remain in the towns as his ancestors had done. He preferred the Field of Rest amongst the marshes and the sandy islets in the shelter of the Nile waters. This was the first realm of Osiris where he lived exactly as he had done during his first life, but without ever growing old.

Later, he departed, crossing the seas, stopping, perhaps, on the Phoenician shore near Byblos and rising up finally into the sky to reside in the Milky Way, between the north and the east, but rather more towards the north. There is his eternal kingdom. The sun and the moon shine at the same time. When it is hot in the middle of the day, the north wind blows to freshen the air. The harvests in this kingdom are plentiful and magnificent. Mighty ramparts protect his dwelling from the threats of Set and from evil spirits. A palace like Pharaoh's, but a thousand times more beautiful, rises up in the centre of delectable gardens. There Osiris, surrounded by his people, led a peaceful life, where all the pleasures of the earthly life could be enjoyed without any of its sorrows.

Nevertheless, Osiris, Ounnefer-the-good, the symbol of perfect goodness, wanted to open the doors of his paradise to his former faithful subjects, those who were the followers of Horus, so that those who had led good lives on earth, who had understood the divine teachings and who had followed the right path, might later lead a blessed existence in the other world and enjoy everlasting happiness near the god whom they had worshipped and honoured during their human life.

3

Horus

SIRIS had not entirely departed this world. Just as the grain sown in the earth in November rises out of the ground in the spring, as the tree develops new branches, as the annual flooding of the Nile wakes the sluggish waters, he had left an offspring. The son of Osiris, like the new corn, like the rejuvenated waters of the Nile, like the bud which bursts forth, was born after the death of his father. Isis gave birth to him in the marshes of Lake Burlos not far from Buto in the Delta, where she had hidden herself in a place called Chemnis in the midst of tall reeds. It was there that she kept him and brought him up in solitude so that no one should know where he was, and also to keep him safe from the plottings and attacks of Set, the wicked one. When he was very young, he went about quite naked, for it was extremely hot in the marshes of the Nile, so he wore only necklets and bracelets chosen for their magical power to keep away all enemies from the little child. His mother, crouched on the ground to be more completely hidden, nursed him on her knees and fed him. He ate what she herself ate, the seeds taken from the papyrus fruit, those great round heads which swayed on the tall stalks, longer than a man's arm.

From time to time, she went as far as the town to spend an entire day begging. She asked charitable people to give her food, and in the evening she would return, and take in her arms Horus her beautiful child, her little golden son. But one evening, looking for him in the papyrus and the bulrushes, she found him lying lifeless on the ground. The ground was soaked with the tears which he had shed and foam was on his lips. The little heart was no longer beating, the limbs were powerless and the pale body was a lifeless corpse.

Isis, the goddess, uttered a great cry of sorrow which shattered the silence; then she burst into loud lamentation, deploring her new misfortune. Now that Horus was dead, who was left to protect her, to take vengeance upon Set, the wicked one? When the people of the nearest village heard her cries, they came running to share her sorrow, and they, too, began to utter loud cries and deep moans. But no matter how much they sympathised, neither their tears nor their cries could bring the divine Horus back to life.

Then a woman stepped forward from the group and came close to Isis, the weeping mother. This woman was well known in the village where she was a big landowner. She tried to console Isis, comforting her and assuring her that it was possible to cure Horus.

"For," she said, "it is a scorpion which has stung him. He has been attacked by the reptile Aunab."

Then Isis leaned over the child to find out whether he was still breathing and she saw the puncture and, looking very closely, she realised that the flesh was poisoned. Taking the child in her arms, she pressed him tightly to her uttering great cries of anguish which echoed far, far away, even to infinity. . . .

At the noise of these terrible lamentations, the goddess Nephthys, sister of Isis and Osiris, ran up, and she also began to wail and weep bitterly, sharing the mother's sorrow. With her came also the goddess of scorpions. Nephthys advised her sister to invoke Ra, the great god, and to beg his help. Isis obeyed. She cried out, she called with all her might, she poured out her despairing supplications and Ra, the sun god, checked his celestial ship in its course through the heavenly river. Everything in the whole earth stopped for an instant. And the god, Thoth, left the boat and descended to the earth, Thoth who possessed the most powerful spells in the whole world.

He approached Isis and questioned her, encouraging her to confide in him.

"What is the matter with him? What is the matter with him, O Isis, O thou the goddess of the spells, O thou whose mouth can utter the most potent of charms. Assuredly, it is not possible that evil can have reached the baby Horus, for he is protected by Ra, the great god. Take comfort, I have left the celestial ship to come and cure your son."

Thus did Thoth dispel the anguish of the mother's heart for he brought with him remedies and healing.

Turning towards the lifeless child, he began to utter magic formulae, saying: "Awaken, Horus, gladden the heart of your mother, Isis, and may our hearts share in

4

her joy! The royal ship of Ra himself, the great god, stopped in its course for the well-being of Horus and of his mother, Isis. Poison drop down into the earth! It is the will of the gods that I, Thoth, should cure the child Horus, that I should bring him back to life for the consolation of his mother, Isis. O Horus, O Horus! Awaken, you must live for your mother's sake."

And little Horus came back to life to gladden the heart of his mother.

Then Thoth went back into the ship of a thousand voyages and it immediately took up again its majestic journey, and, from one end of the sky to the other, all the gods rejoiced in their hearts.

Returned to life, Horus continued to grow, hidden among the bulrushes and the giant papyrus. He learnt to read books and he studied on a roll of papyrus, spread out on his knees, to learn to decipher the sacred signs.

He grew up thus and Osiris came back to the earth to arm his son and to prepare him for battle. He asked him: "What is the most splendid action in the life of a man?" And Horus replied without hesitation, "To avenge his father and his mother upon those who have made them suffer harm."

Then Osiris decided to offer his son the help of an animal to aid him in his contests, and he asked Horus to choose between a lion and a horse as companion. And Horus preferred a horse. "Because," he said, "a lion is good against cowards, but a horse allows its rider to pursue his enemies." Then Osiris, reassured, returned to live peacefully in the other world.

Horus concentrated all his energy on avenging his father. He put on white sandals to cross the country. He gathered around him the Egyptians who had remained faithful to Osiris and were confident that they had, as their leader, the rightful son of Osiris. They were sometimes called the followers of Horus, and sometimes the servants of Horus. Amongst them were warriors armed with bows and arrows, and others armed with boomerangs, led by the wolf, Oupouat, whose symbol was crossed with a club. They lost no time in attacking Set's demons. The latter, surprised by the attack, changed themselves first into gazelles, then into crocodiles, and finally into serpents—all the hateful animals devoted to Set. For three days, they strove against each other.

Isis, impatient and anxious, intervened to help her son, but Horus, infuriated, turned on her like a panther and began to chase her. She escaped from him, but he ran after her, caught up with her and, in his rage, tore off her royal coronet. But Thoth saw everything, and he gave her a helmet like a cow's head, so that Isis and her companion, Hathor, often seemed to be one and the same person.

This war has never come to an end, for the battle continues to rage with neither combatant being the victor. In exasperation, the gods summoned the two rivals before their tribunal, and both of them agreed to accept as arbitrator, Thoth, the lord of Hermopolis.

Set was the first to plead, and he claimed that Horus could not be considered the legitimate son of Osiris because he was born after the latter's death. But Horus proved in his turn that the reasoning of Set was false, and Thoth ordered Set to return the heritage of Osiris to the young Horus. The gods ratified this judgment. Sibou, ancestor of the two pleaders, intervened in his turn; he divided Egypt in two. Set was to have the Valley of the Nile between Memphis and the First Cataract; Horus received the Delta. Thus was the heritage of Sibou, which his children were not wise enough to preserve, cut in two. It was not until later that the Pharaohs united the two kingdoms, and this is why they wear the red crown of the north, surmounted by the white helmet, which is the symbol of the kings of the south.

Some say that Horus received the whole of Egypt, whereas Set was relegated to Nubia, the red country, and the western desert. This would explain why the inhabitants of these regions have always been enemies of the Egyptians. For neither Thoth's judgment nor the settlement of Sibou put an end to the struggle. Horus and his followers continued to fight Set and his confederates, the hideous monsters, hippopotamuses, crocodiles and wild boars. One of these battles is told in its entirety along the walls of the Temple of Edfu.

Vanquished, the hordes of Set retreated towards the north. But they returned to the attack and, in a terrible mêlée, the bulls of Horus and the donkeys of Set confronted each other. Horus the sorcerer was first in the combat. One day, he turned himself into a hawk, so that he could fight on the back of a hippopotamus, which was none other than Set himself, but the latter changed into a gazelle and disappeared before Horus, who had now become a falcon, could catch him. Another day, to frighten his enemy, Horus took the form of a lion with a human head, with claws as sharp as knives. But Set always escaped.

His companions, however, grew weary of the struggle. They could be seen in the Gulf of Suez returning to the deserts of Nubia. They believed themselves inviolate in the sea, their element. Nevertheless, Horus pursued them, catching up with them in the Red Sea and swiftly dispersing them. Then he returned to Edfu to celebrate his victory.

From that time onwards, Horus was the lawful master of the land of Egypt. And after him reigned his descendants: Menes, who was the first king of the first dynasty of men, then the long line of Pharaohs of all the Egyptian dynasties.

However, Set was not dead, and at every hour of the day the struggle goes on between the followers of Horus, god of the light, and the servants of Set, god of the darkness. And each time that the sun triumphs over the darkness and storm clouds of Set, men celebrate the victory of the valiant Horus.

4

The Story of Two Brothers

N the land of Egypt there were two brothers; they were the children of the same mother and the same father.

The elder was called Anpu; he had a wife and he owned a house. As for the younger brother, Bata, it was he who wove the cloth; he who walked behind the herds as he took them to the fields; he who spun the thread; he who tilled, who dug, who weeded, harvested and thrashed the corn. He was a good farmer who had no rival in the land of Egypt.

And every day Bata returned from the fields, walking behind his cows, bearing a heavy burden of hay for the cattle to eat during the night. He used to place this load in front of his brother who was sitting with his wife, and then went into the stable with the cows, ate, drank and went to sleep. When the skies lightened and another day had dawned, he baked the loaves and put them in front of his brother, who gave him his share of the bread to take to the fields. Then the younger man drove the cows to the pastures, and, as he walked behind them, the cows said to him: "The grass is good in that place". He listened to what they had to say and took them to the good pasturage which they desired. And then the cows which were with him became fine-looking fat creatures and had little calves.

One day, during the ploughing season, his elder brother said to Bata, "Get the plough ready, so that we can begin work, for the floods have receded, the water has drained away and it is time to plough. We will begin our task tomorrow."

The young brother did all that his elder brother told him to do. When the next day dawned, they went to the fields with their plough and they worked, and they worked, and they worked, throughout the whole day without stopping to rest, and their toil filled them with happiness. And after many days spent in this manner they were still in the fields hoeing up the ground. Then Anpu, the elder brother, called his younger brother Bata, and said to him: "Run into the village and bring us some seed."

The young brother returned to the house, where he found his sister-in-law busy dressing her hair. She was re-braiding the innumerable little tight plaits which took several hours to arrange on her head and were then left untouched for a long time. The young man said to her: "Get up and give me the seed, so that I can take it back to the fields immediately, for my elder brother told me not to tarry."

Without bothering to move, the woman said: "Go yourself and open the earthenware bin and take what you like, for I am not going to interrupt my hairdressing to wait on you."

Then Bata went into the stable, chose an enormous jar, for he meant to take a large quantity, filled it with wheat and barley, and went out, bending under the weight.

As he passed the woman asked him: "How much have you taken?" and he replied: "Three measures of barley, two measures of wheat, as much as my shoulders can carry." Then Anpu's wife declared: "You have plenty of spirit; every day I notice how you become stronger and stronger," and she looked at him admiringly.

Suddenly she stood up, and said to him, "You are stronger than your elder brother, I ought to have married you." Bata, enraged like a leopard from the south, because she was criticising her husband, turned on her and accused her of making wicked suggestions. She was so afraid that she began immediately to think of some means of getting rid of him.

Bata lifted up his burden again and set off for the fields. When he joined his elder brother, they resumed their work. When evening fell and Anpu returned to his house, the younger brother took the cattle to the stable and brought back his tools.

Frightened, because of what she had suggested, the woman had taken a cloth and some grease, and had made marks on her skin like those caused by the attack of a bandit. When her husband arrived home as usual that evening, he found his wife lying down and sad; she did not pour water over his hands as usual, nor did she light a lamp for him; the house was dark and she was stretched out, all dishevelled.

Then her husband said to her: "What has happened?" and this is what she replied: "It is your younger brother. When he came to fetch the seed for you, finding me alone, he began to speak ill of you and to say that I should have married him instead, but I would not listen to him, I reminded him that you were like a father to him. Then he was afraid and he beat me black and blue so that I should not tell you what he had done. If you let this man live, I shall kill myself, for if he learns that I have told you of his wicked deeds, what may he not do to me?"

The elder brother then leapt up like a leopard of the south. He sharpened his knife well and gripped it in his hand. He stood behind the door of the stable ready to kill his brother.

When, at sunset, the younger man arrived, as he always did, heavily burdened with hay and driving the beasts before him, the leading cow said to him, just before entering: "Look out for your elder brother who is lying in wait behind the door with a knife to kill you. Fly for your life." He heard what she said and then the second cow in her turn repeated the same thing: "Take care; your elder brother is behind the door waiting to kill you with his knife." Bata stooped down and looked beneath the door and saw his brother's feet as he stood with the knife in his hand. He dropped his bundle of hay and began to run as fast as his legs would carry him, but his brother rushed out in pursuit of him, the knife still clutched in his hand.

Then Bata called upon Ra-Horus, the sun who journeys from one horizon in the morning to the other in the evening, saying: "My good master, it is you who judge between the just and the unjust." Ra heard his cry and made an immense flood of water, full of crocodiles, to appear between him and his brother. One brother was upon one side, the other upon the other. The elder brother tried twice to reach the younger and strike him, but he could not. From the opposite bank his brother hailed him and said: "Stay where you are until it is light upon the earth. When the circle of the sun rises above the horizon I will plead with you before him so as to arrive at the truth, but I shall never be with you again. I shall never again be in the place where you are. I shall go to the Valley of the Acacias."

When the earth was filled with light and the next day had come, each brother saw the other. Bata spoke to Anpu saying: "Why did you come up behind me to kill me treacherously without having heard what I had to say? I am your brother and you are like a father to me. Well, when you sent me to fetch the grain, your wife said to me: 'You are stronger than your elder brother.' I did not reply and that remark was twisted for you into something different."

Then Bata took an oath by Ra-Horus, saying: "To think you are capable of hiding with a dagger in your hand, so as to kill me treacherously. What baseness, what infamy!"

So saying, he took up a sickle, and gave himself a great gaping wound, and collapsed fainting. Anpu cursed his own heart and remained there weeping. He sprang forward, but could not cross to the bank where his brother stood because of the crocodiles.

Then the younger brother hailed him and said, "So whilst I was being accused of having spoken ill of you,

you did not think of any of the good things I had done.
Ah, go back to your house, look after your animals yourself, for I shall never again live in the place where you
live. I shall go to the Valley of the Acacias, and this is
what will happen. I shall tear out my heart by magic and
I shall put it high up in the Acacia blossom, and when the
Acacia is cut and my heart falls to the ground, you will
come and find it.

"Do not be discouraged if it takes you seven years of
searching; but once you have found it, put it in a jar
of fresh water and I will live again to avenge the evil
that would have been done to me. Now, if the beer
in the pitcher which is put into your hand throws up
froth, or if the wine which you are given becomes cloudy,
you will know that something has happened to me.
Do not fail to set off immediately because I shall have
need of you." And he departed for the Valley of the
Acacias.

Anpu returned to his house, his hand on his head, his
forehead covered with dust as a sign of mourning. Then
he killed his wife and threw her body to the dogs and
lived in mourning for his younger brother.

Later, many, many days later, the younger brother
took up his abode in the Valley of the Acacias. He spent
his days hunting the beasts of the desert, and at night he
used to sleep under the Acacia tree where on the topmost
blossom his heart was lying. With his own hands, he
made a well-stocked farm in the Valley of the Acacias, so
as to have a roof over his head and a house to live in.

One day, when he came out of his house, he encoun-
tered the Enneads, the nine gods who were setting out to
administer their Land of Egypt. The nine gods spoke all

at once, saying: "Oh Bata, are you not lonely here after having left your country because of your elder brother's wife? See now, he has killed his wife and you are avenged." Their hearts suffered for him, seeing him living alone, and Ra-Horus said to Khnum, the sculptor of children's bodies: "Oh, make a wife for Bata, so that he shall no longer be alone."

Khnum made him a companion to live with—the most beautiful of all the women in the Land of Egypt. The seven Hathors came to see her and predicted that she would die by the sword.

Bata loved her dearly, very dearly. She remained in the house whilst all day long he hunted the animals of the desert to place them at her feet at night. He said to her, "Do not venture outside, for fear that the Nile should swallow you up. You would not be able to escape because you are only a woman. As for me, my heart is lying on the topmost blossom of the Acacia tree and if anyone else finds it, I must fight with him." Then he confided in her all that had happened to his heart.

Many days later, Bata had set off to hunt as usual; his wife had gone out to stroll under the Acacia which shaded the house. She saw the River Nile, who was sending his waves towards her, and she began to run and took shelter in her house. But the River Nile cried out to the Acacia: "If only I could have her," and the Acacia gave him a tress of her hair.

This lock was carried by the Nile as far as Egypt; and the river left it in the washing-place of the Pharaoh's laundresses. The scent of the lock of hair impregnated the Pharaoh's linen and the laundresses were scolded: "There is a smell of ointment in the king's linen." Every day they were scolded more and more until they did not know what they were doing.

Then the overseer of Pharaoh's laundresses went to the washing-place himself, for he was disgusted at the reproaches hurled at him every day. He stopped and stood before the water just in front of the lock of hair. He made someone climb into the water and bring it to him. Finding it smelt very good, he took it to Pharaoh. The royal sorcerers were sent for and they said to their master: "This tress of hair belongs to a daughter of Ra-Horus who is divine. Since it is a homage which comes to you from a strange land, send out messengers into all the Land Beyond to find this creature; send many men with the messenger who goes to the Valley of Acacias, so that they may bring her back." And His Majesty declared: "That is perfect, perfect," and he despatched the messengers.

After many more days, the men who had gone to the Land Beyond came to give their report to His Majesty. The only ones who did not return were those sent to the Valley of the Acacias: Bata had killed them. He had spared only one to make his report to His Majesty. When the Pharaoh heard what had happened, he sent a large number of men and archers, and even soldiers with war chariots, to bring back this creature; there was even a woman servant to keep her company and help her to dress. They brought her back and rejoiced to see her in the Land of Egypt. His Majesty loved her dearly, so dearly that she became his Favourite. They made her tell them about her husband, and she explained that if they cut down the Acacia tree, he would be destroyed. Then men and archers were sent with their tools to cut down the tree. They cut off the blossom on which the heart of Bata was lying, and he fell dead at that unlucky moment.

When the second day dawned, after the Acacia had been cut down, Anpu, the elder brother of Bata, went into his house and sat down after washing his hands. He was served with a pitcher of beer which frothed over. Then he was given another of wine which clouded over. He seized his sandals, his stick, his clothes and his weapons and set off at once towards the Valley of Acacias. He went into his younger brother's house and found Bata stretched out dead on the bed. He set out at once to find the heart of his brother, beneath the Acacia tree, in the shade of which he had slept each night. Anpu searched and searched for three whole years, wearing himself out and finding nothing. He had broken into the fourth year when, obeying the desire of his heart to return to Egypt, he said to himself: "I shall depart from here tomorrow." When the dawn lighted up the land, he went back to the Acacia tree once more and spent the day searching beneath it. In the evening, just as he was going home, when he was still looking around him, he found a seed which he picked up. It was his brother's heart. He brought a cup of fresh water and dropped the seed into it, and then sat down, as was his daily custom. When night fell, the heart having absorbed the water, Bata trembled in all his limbs and began to gaze upon his brother. Anpu took the cup of fresh water in which was his brother's heart, and gave it to his brother to drink. Immediately the heart slipped back into its place, and Bata returned to his original self.

The brothers embraced and talked together like two

good friends. At last, Bata said to his elder brother: "I shall become a great bull, who will have all the good signs, the sacred signs—a black pelt, a white triangle on the forehead, a winged vulture spread on its back, the likeness of a scarab on its tongue, and all the hair of its tail double. You will sit on my back when dawn breaks and, when we arrive at the place where my wife is, I will take my revenge. You must lead me to the sacred place, and you will be heaped with silver and gold for having brought Pharaoh such a great miracle, and everyone will rejoice in the Land of Egypt. Then you can return home."

And when the light of the following day spread its radiance upon the land, Bata changed himself into a bull just as he had foretold. At dawn, Anpu, his elder brother, jumped on to his back and they hurried to the destined place. When they showed the bull to His Majesty, he examined it—recognising all the signs—and rejoiced greatly, saying: "A miracle has occurred." And the Land of Egypt rejoiced because of the bull.

The elder brother was loaded with silver and gold and went back to his village. As for the bull, it was installed with plenty of servants and comforts, for Pharaoh prized it dearly.

Many days later, the bull, ambling along (for sacred animals roamed free), went into the harem and stopped in front of the Favourite, and began talking to her, saying: "Look at me. I am still alive." She replied: "Who are you then?" and he answered: "I am Bata. You know very well that when you told Pharaoh to cut down the Acacia it would do me harm and stop me from living; but look at me—I am still alive." He went out of the harem, and the Favourite of Pharaoh was afraid of what her husband had said.

His Majesty, having spent a happy day with his Favourite, summoned her to his table and was most gracious and affectionate towards her; so she asked him "Swear to me by Amon-Ra and say 'Whatsoever you ask of me I will grant'." He consented, and she went on to say: "I wish to eat the liver of this bull."

There was great consternation in the court of Pharaoh, for the animal was sacred, but when the next day dawned, a great feast was held, with offerings and sacrifices in honour of the bull. Eventually one of the chief butchers of the Pharaoh was sent to slaughter it.

Now, after the butcher had killed the bull, and whilst it was still weighing heavily upon the shoulders of those who were carrying it away, it let fall two drops of blood near His Majesty's double flight of steps. One fell on one side of the great entrance to Pharaoh's Palace, and the other fell opposite, and from these two drops there sprang up two tall persimmon trees, each of great beauty. They were splendid trees with wonderful fruit like golden apples, about which the proverb is written: "One mouthful of persimmon comforts the heart."

Speedily His Majesty was informed: "There is a strange miracle for Your Majesty. Two great persimmon trees have grown up before the portal of the royal palace." And all in the Land of Egypt rejoiced at this wonder, and offerings were made as to sacred trees.

Several days later, His Majesty put on his diadem of lapis lazuli and hung garlands of all sorts of flowers round his neck. He climbed into his scarlet chariot to go out of the palace and see these miraculous persimmon trees.

The woman asked Bata: "How much have you taken?"

The Favourite also left the palace in a chariot drawn by two horses and followed behind Pharaoh. His Majesty sat down under one of the persimmons, the Favourite under the other. When she was seated, the persimmon said to his wife: "Ah treacherous one! I am Bata and I live although ill treated by you. You knew perfectly well that to ask Pharaoh to cut down the Acacia was doing me harm; you knew perfectly well that to slaughter the bull was to kill me."

After several more days, when the Favourite was seated at table with Pharaoh and His Majesty was well disposed towards her, she said to him: "Take an oath by Amon-Ra saying: 'Whatsoever you ask of me I will grant it'." He agreed to her request, so she continued: "Cut down the two trees and have beautiful caskets made from the wood."

His Majesty granted her wish and sent skilful carpenters to cut down the trees, whilst the royal wife, the Favourite, stood by watching. As she watched, a chip of wood suddenly flew into her mouth. The carpenters made the caskets and did everything she wished.

Many days later, the Favourite gave birth to a son and His Majesty was told: "You have a son born to you." They brought the child to him, and he was given nurses and servants, and everyone rejoiced in the entire Land of Egypt.

One day, a fete was held in the child's honour. His Majesty loved him dearly, so dearly, and he was greeted as the royal son, Prince Kaoushou. Later His Majesty made him heir to the throne of the Land of Egypt.

After many years, His Majesty died and flew away into the heavens. The new Pharaoh said: "Bring before me the chief officers of His Majesty that I may tell them my story." They brought his former wife and he judged her before them and the councillors approved his judgment; they brought his elder brother to him and he made him heir to the entire Land of Egypt. Bata was King of Egypt for twenty years. When he departed this life, his elder brother occupied his place from the day of the funeral ceremonies.

5

The Complaints of the Fellah

I N the distant past, there lived in the Salt Plain a man named Kounoupou, with his wife, his children, his donkeys and his dogs. He earned his living as a merchant, carrying goods to the town from the Salt Plain, and exchanging them for corn and millet.

This man said to his wife one day: "I am going into Egypt to try to earn money to pay for our children's food. Come and measure the wheat which is left in the granary from this year's harvest."

They measured eight bushels of grain and the man said to his wife:

"Here are two bushels of corn to feed your children. With the remaining six bushels of corn make me bread and beer, so that I may eat for as long as my journey lasts."

When all was ready, the fellah set off for Egypt. He loaded his donkeys with bundles of reeds and bulrushes to make matting; on their backs he piled natron which is used in embalming mummies, a large quantity of salt, acacia wood from the Country of Oxen, wolf skins, wild cat skins, onyx, talc, bags of coriander seed and aniseed, grapes, pigeons, partridges, quails, bunches of anemones and narcissus, sunflower seeds and pimentoes. He was well loaded with all the good things produced in the Salt Plain.

Then this fellah journeyed towards the south, to Henassieh, and when he reached the place called Pafifi to the north of the town of Madenit, at the entrance of Fayyum, he met a man standing on the banks of the Nile. This man was a certain Tehouti, son of Asari, both serfs of a steward at the Royal Palace, the celebrated Maroui-tensi.

This Tehouti shouted out as soon as he saw the donkeys which were so heavily laden with interesting-looking bundles: "O master, my god, my protector, look favourably upon me that I may succeed in getting possession of all those good things."

Now the dwelling of Tehouti was built on the side of the road which bordered the Nile. The path was narrow at this point and so cramped that there was only a space the size of a piece of cloth between the water on one side and a field of corn on the other, so the merchant was obliged to make his donkeys walk in single file one behind the other. This took some little time.

Tehouti seized this opportunity to say to his slave: "Run to the house and bring me a piece of linen."

Almost immediately the slave returned with the piece of linen, unfolded it and then spread it right in the centre of the path so that the selvedge touched the edge of the water and the fringe reached the field of corn. The fellah came jolting along the road driving his donkeys in front of him one by one; they advanced slowly because they were so heavily laden. The peasant was not in the least worried for he was on the right of way.

Then Tehouti stopped him, saying, "Take care, you; do not let your donkeys trample on my linen."

The peasant replied "I will not spoil your linen which is drying there; I can easily pass to one side."

And he drove the leading donkey to the side of the field.

But then Tehouti said to him, "Does my corn have to act as a path for you, fellah?"

The peasant retorted: "I must get by somehow. One side of the road is sown with corn, you have barred the middle way with your linen, and the slope of the bank prevents me from passing beside the river. What do you expect me to do?"

While they were arguing, the foremost donkey stretched out his neck and swallowed a mouthful of corn. Then Tehouti cried out: "Hey, you, since your donkey is eating my corn, I will seize him as damages and I will put him to work; he looks strong enough."

The peasant was angry. "I follow the road which is free to everyone and to avoid making trouble, I move to one side, and now you want to take my donkey for a mouthful of corn."

Once started, nothing would stop him, and he continued: "Let me tell you, I know the master of this estate. He is the high steward of the Place, Marouitensi; it is certainly he who hunts down thieves and casts them out of this Land of Egypt. You will not make me believe that I can be robbed on such lands."

Tehouti replied: "It is I who am speaking to you and yet you reply by referring to Maroui, the steward at the Palace. You change the subject."

At this point he stopped arguing, broke off a green branch of tamarisk, beat the poor fellow with it, and threw him to the ground. After this he took off the donkeys, drove them into his yard and carefully closed the gate.

The poor fellah began to weep bitterly and to cry out loudly because of his smarting back and all the harm he had suffered.

At the sound of all this noise, Tehouti returned, jeering at him and giving him good advice: "Don't raise your voice, you, or I will soon despatch you to the realms of silence, and you will not cry out so loudly because you will be dead."

The poor peasant replied: "You have beaten me, you have robbed me and now you want to thrust my words down my throat. Give me back my donkeys, or I shall see that your bad name is made known everywhere."

For four whole days, the peasant uttered complaints and threats in the ears of Tehouti, but nothing had any effect. Tehouti would not give in; he seemed not to hear.

On the fifth day, the fellah went off to the town to lodge his complaint before the Palace steward, Marouitensi. When he arrived, the steward was just leaving his house to get into his boat and go on a tour of inspection. The peasant stood in front of him and said: "Oh, allow me to make my petition to you or, if you are in a hurry, let me make it to one of your confidential attendants."

The Palace steward sent him to his official and the peasant told him all that had happened in great detail, and left him very well informed about the crime.

When Marouitensi returned, the official made his report and told him the whole story. Before deciding anything, the steward, Maroui, consulted his friends and asked them if they knew this Tehouti. They replied: "Just a minute, are we sure that it was Tehouti who stole the donkeys? Might it not have been his slave who did it without his knowledge? And what is there to prove that the fellah ever had the goods or the donkeys? These peasants are always squabbling and making accusations."

One of Maroui's friends added: "You are never going to punish Tehouti just for a peasant's story? A little natron and a little salt is nothing to make such a fuss about. Let him be told quite simply that he must return what he has taken from the fellah if, indeed, he has taken anything."

Marouitensi kept silent. He did not reply either to the peasant or to his friends who advised him, but he reflected.

The next day, the peasant presented himself in person before Maroui. Without being in the least intimidated by such an important person, he addressed him and said, "O my lord, you who are great among the great ones. I know very well who you are. You are responsible for going down the canal in a boat which belongs to Pharaoh, and from it you keep watch over men. I know that you administer justice: you are the father of the poor, the protector of the widow, the tutor of the orphan. I should like to be able to say that your name is greater than the best of laws. Be just to me. Return me my donkeys and my merchandise."

By then the steward Marouitensi had finished thinking.

He went to pay court to the Pharaoh, King Nabka, the king who was called the Just, and he said to him: "My lord, I have heard the complaint of one of these fellahin who understand so well how to put their case. He is only a poor peasant, but he is as eloquent as ten lawyers! He claims to have been robbed by one of my farmers. He concocts such splendid phrases that it would be an entertainment for Your Majesty to hear him plead."

The King replied: "Marouitensi, my friend, if you want me to be in a good humour, let this affair take a long time. I should be very much amused by this personage. We must see how long he will go on without getting tired, and we must hear all the speeches that he is capable of making. Do not reply to any of his complaints, but come and repeat to me everything he manages to say. You have only to write down all that he says. Nevertheless, you must see that his wife and his children are looked after during all this time. Someone must be sent to till his land, cultivate his garden and take his place in the house. As for him, arrange that he shall be given food to eat without his knowing who sends it."

And all this was done. The peasant was allowed four loaves and two pitchers of beer every day. Marouitensi had them sent by a friend who gave the impression that he was interested in the poor fellow out of charity. And the governor of the Salt Plain received instructions that he was to send a daily ration of bread to the fellah's wife, and at least three measures of corn had to be used in baking it.

Having carried out Pharaoh's orders, Maroui awaited events. The fellah soon came back to complain again.

"O steward of the Palace, my master, you who are a governor sent to us from the skies. Do not be diverted from the path of justice. Do not allow anyone to be robbed. If your judgment falters, if the balance of justice be false, the villagers will become thieves, the police will no longer arrest the guilty and evil and wrongdoing will sweep into the town like a flood."

The steward of the Palace, Maroui, interrupted him to ask: "Then you think it very important that my farmer should be punished? You insist upon it?"

The fellah replied: "If he who should respect the law robs, who then will follow up the criminals? Eventually your own turn will come. These rascals will tear down your vines, destroy your farmyard. They will kill the wildfowl which swarm in your ponds. Think of your own interests."

And he went on like this for some time, repeating the same prayers in twenty different forms, not stopping until Maroui turned his back upon him.

He was soon back again for the third time, when he said: "Steward of the Palace, you should check theft, you should protect the poor. Take care, for the next life is approaching. Oh, how many times are you going to let us be eaten by the crocodiles without listening to our cries?" And he compared Maroui to the bird of prey which eats the little sparrows, and to the cook, happy to kill so that no animal should escape, and so on, for hours at a time, without noticing the scribe hidden behind the terrace wall, carefully noting his words.

Exasperated with listening to all this, Maroui sent two of his servants armed with sticks to beat the peasant, so as to teach him to hold his tongue.

But he began all over again: "His eyes are blind, he is dead, he is like a policeman who leads robbers and brigands, he is . . . he is . . ." Under the repeated blows, rubbing his sore back, he finally went away.

But he came back to lodge his complaint a fourth time, and he put himself right in the path of the steward when he came back from his morning devotions at the temple of Amon, and started to declaim: "O blessed one, blessed of the gods, he who comes out of the temple in the morning and who allows the wicked to increase throughout the realm. O listen to what I keep on repeating. The prayers of the unfortunate will be your undoing. You are like the hunter who thinks of nothing but of throwing himself upon his prey: he harpoons the hippopotamus: he pierces the flesh of wild bulls with arrows: he spreads the net to trap the birds: and he never spares a minute to pity his victims."

Maroui managed to get past the pleader, and the fellah had to give up putting forward his case any more that morning. But nothing would stop him from coming back to plead a fifth time, when he began all over again his interminable discourse, never stopping for a moment, saying again the same things, but always finding new ways of putting them, and of describing his misery and the indifference of the steward, and the consequences of injustice in this world and the next.

The sixth time, he compared Maroui to men who catch fish. "You depopulate the countryside as fishermen depopulate the river. You take what you want from the unfortunate when you ought to protect them."

A seventh time he came back, and as usual he found plenty of words to express his indignation. He reproached the steward for his injustice and his harshness, with an eloquence which was ceaselessly renewed.

Faced with the hopelessness of these harangues, one might have thought he would have given up the project, but no, he came back even an eighth time.

"You steal! and it is for nothing! There is no point in it! You have a house furnished with everything that you could desire. Your stomach is full, but you take from others all the same: you inspire fear and you believe that in the end fear will stop my pleading. But when you walk towards the tribunal of Osiris you will lose your way, you will never cross the water in the enchanted ferry, you will never reach the bank destined for the just. You did not listen to my pleading when I came to put my case before you, but you will meet me again in the next world, when I shall prefer a charge against you before Anubis! Do not imagine that you are master of the future. Tomorrow will bring fresh happenings and, who knows, tomorrow you may belong to the demons."

And the next day Marouitensi, the steward of the Palace, decided that the game had lasted long enough. He sent two of his slaves to fetch the fellah and bring him before him, but the peasant was now on his guard.

Learning from past experience and expecting blows from a stick, he would not go, but said: "This reminds me of the story of a man who was thirsty and had nothing but his salt tears with which to quench his thirst. It is one of those affairs where he who waits achieves nothing, and where one meets nothing but death."

Maroui had to come in person to see him and say: "Ah, my friend, I sent them to fetch you so that you could live with me at my expense."

The fellah agreed to go and this was the tenth time that he had presented himself before the steward. But this time it was recompense after suffering and when he understood this, he declared: "Can I live for ever, eating your bread and drinking your beer?"

Then the steward replied: "Come here and repeat a little of what you have said during the time you have been pleading your case."

The scribe who had noted down all the innumerable words of the fellah was able to verify the truth of everything he said. He recopied the interminable discourses of the loquacious fellah on a new roll of papyrus without omitting a single complaint, nor a single one of the oft-repeated accusations.

Then this long recital of complaints was sent to Pharaoh Nebka and read out to him, which amused him greatly to begin with until he wearied of this never-ceasing complaint and ended by saying to the steward: "Judge this case yourself and let that be the end of it."

Then the Palace steward, Marouitensi, sent for a clerk of the court, and an official edict was written, signed and countersigned, by which he gave the fellah six slaves and quantities of corn and an abundant supply of millet as well as donkeys and dogs and enough to live on in comfort for the rest of his days with his wife and his children.

On the other hand, it was finally decided that Tehouti should be severely beaten in his turn; and further, he had to return the donkeys and the goods to the fellah.

The bunches of flowers were completely dried up, but one of the donkeys had a little donkey, so that at the end of the affair, the fellah lost nothing by the adventure. On the contrary!

And the fellah, at last satisfied, gave up coming to plead before Marouitensi; he went off to join his wife and his children who had been patiently waiting for him in their little house in the Salt Plain.

6

The Adventures of Sinuhi

INUHI, the friend of Pharaoh, the administrator of the royal estates and his lieutenant over the Bedouin, Sinuhi, the King's right hand, tells the following story:

I am the devoted servant who follows his master, Amenemhat, my king. He whose tomb is in the pyramid of Quanofir entrusted me with his daughter, Princess and heir, and I watch over her in the royal harem. My noble mistress is called Nofrit; she is the favourite wife of King Sanou.

In the year XXX, in the third month of Iakhouit at the time when the god, Ra, was reaching his second horizon, the King Amenemhat, father of my Princess, died on this earth, and his soul soared up into the heavens to join the sun and to return to his creator. The palace was silent as a sign of mourning. The great double portal had been sealed, the courtiers remained crouching, their heads bowed on their knees. The people were utter-ing loud lamentations.

His Majesty, the dead King, had, during his lifetime, sent a great army to make war upon the country of Timihou, the country of Berber tribes who dwelt in the desert of Libya. His eldest son, Prince Sanou, was in command of this army. He had been told to conquer the foreign countries and reduce the Berbers to slavery. Victorious, he had already started on the road for home, taking with him the Berber prisoners, and so many herds that he could not count them.

Since the death of the King, the guardians of the harem, who were friends of the King chosen from amongst the courtiers and officials, sent a number of men towards the west to inform the King's son of the happen-ings at the Palace. The messengers reached him at mid-night and the Prince acted at once. Like a royal falcon, he flew off with his attendants to join those at the palace who were mourning the loss of his father; but the order was given to the Princes of the blood royal to say nothing and to keep the death of the King a secret from the army.

Well, I was present and I even heard the voice of the messenger announcing this grave news, and so my life was at stake; for I should have been held responsible for the slightest leakage of information about a secret which I should never have heard.

I got away as quickly as possible, my heart bursting, and fear attacking all my limbs. I was in despair, and wandered round and round, seeking a place where I might hide. I slipped between two bushes to avoid the well-trodden road which the royal cortège was following. I wended my way towards the south, but I did not wish to return to the royal palace, because I imagined that war had already broken out. It is seldom, indeed, that the Crown Prince appointed by Pharaoh occupies the throne without having to fight against his less favoured and jealous brothers, who always wish to seize his inheritance.

Driven on by fear, I crossed the Canal of the Two Truths at the place called the Sycomore and I arrived at the island of Sneferu and I spent the day there cowering in a field. At dawn I set off again.

I walked throughout the whole day and the night, and early the next day I reached Peten and I rested on an island. Then thirst began to torment me. I was gasping and my throat was contracted. I felt faint and I was already saying to myself, "It is a foretaste of death." Then my heart regained its courage, I pulled my limbs together to raise myself up. I heard cattle lowing. I was near the Bedouin's encampment, and they saw me, and one of their sheiks, who had lived in my district of Egypt, recognised me. He gave me some water and boiled me some milk. After this I journeyed along with him and his tribe, passing from country to country, until I reached a region of Syria, where I remained for a year and a half.

Then the Prince of Syria, Amu, ordered me to appear before him, and said: "You will be happy with me for you will hear talk of Egypt." He said this because he knew who I was. Egyptian exiles had spoken to him about me. He began to question me. "Why have you come here? What induced you to leave your own country? What has happened in the palace of Amenemhat, King of the Two Egypts?"

Realising that he believed I had been involved in some

The poor fellah began to weep bitterly

plot against the King, I replied artfully: "Yes, certainly something has happened. When I returned from an expedition into the Berber country, I heard a secret which was not intended for my ears. My heart was overwhelmed with fear, terror made me flee into the desert. However, I was not blamed, no one spat in my face, no one called me evil names. I do not know what brought me to this country rather than another; it must have been the divine will of Amon-Ra."

But Amu pressed me further. "What will happen to Egypt now it has lost its protector? Amenemhat was respected in foreign countries as much as the goddess Sokhit herself, who has the power to send a plague upon the earth when she wishes to do so."

I let him read my thoughts and then I said, "Amon-Ra has had pity upon us. The son of Amenemhat has entered the palace and has already taken up his heritage. Certainly he is a master of wisdom, prudent in his plans, kindly in his decisions, and he understands how to command. Even during his father's lifetime, he subdued foreign nations, whilst his brother remained inside the palace. He is a valiant man, indeed, who throws himself into the struggle and attacks the Berbers. He runs so swiftly that the fugitive who speeds before him cannot escape. He never grows weary of fight. If he meets resistance, he reaches for his weapons, overthrows his adversary and kills him with the first thrust. No one has ever succeeded in turning aside his spear, no one but he can draw back his bow.

"The city loves him and he is called the well-beloved, the most gracious of men. The women go about singing his praises. He is King. Amon-Ra gave him to us and the land rejoices to be his and to live under his rule. He will conquer the countries of the south, and he does not fear those of the north. It is to be hoped that he holds your name in good esteem, for if he takes it into his head to send an expedition here, he will know how to treat you as you deserve. He is ever ready to be fair and just to a country which submits to his rule."

The head of the country of Syria answered me: "Assuredly, Egypt is fortunate in realising the value of her Prince! As for you, since you are here, stay with me and I will see that you prosper."

He treated me better than his own children, he gave me his eldest daughter in marriage and he offered me a choice of the richest of his lands on the frontier, in the pleasant region of Aia. There, figs and grapes ripen; wine is more abundant than water; there is plenty of honey and olive oil; and all kinds of fruit-trees abound. Barley and wheat grow in profusion, and there is un-limited flour, as well as all kinds of cattle. I was given special privileges when the Prince appointed me as ruler of a tribe. Every day I was allotted a ration of bread and of wine, of boiled meat and roast fowl and game. Cakes of all kinds were brought to me, as well as milk.

I spent many, many years there. My sons became valiant men, each one chief of his tribe. As for me, I heartily welcomed whoever passed through my estates and, remembering how I, myself, had been a fugitive, I gave water to the thirsty, I put the lost traveller on the right road again, I welcomed and comforted those who had been attacked by robbers. My hospitality, in fact, be-came so far famed that everyone wished to stay with me. For some years, I was in charge of the soldiers entrusted with defending the Prince of Syria against those Bedouin who were bold enough to attack us. And when I marched swiftly against a country with my soldiers, the whole land trembled to its depths. I took the cattle, I carried off the serfs, and commandeered the slaves. I slaughtered the men-at-arms.

By my sword-blade, by my bow, by my forced marches, by my well-conceived plans, I gained the heart of my prince and he loved me when he saw my bravery. He put his children under my orders when he realised the strength of my arm.

One day, there arrived a Syrian who was the strongest of the strong. He challenged me in my tent. As a hero he stood alone, for he had vanquished all the strong men of the country. He said that he would enter into single combat with me and that he would strip me of all my wealth. He even went so far as to say out loud that he would take my herds and drive them into his own land and distribute them among his tribe.

The Prince consulted with me and I said: "I know nothing of this man. I have never been in his tent, because I am not an ally of his. He pursues me out of pure jealousy because he sees that I am in your service. May the god Amon-Ra help us! I was a beggar, I have become a chief. I was a nomad, and now I have my status with the peasants: no wonder he does not like me. Well then, if he has a heart for this fight, may Amon-Ra decide between us."

I spent the night bending my bow, sharpening my arrows and flexing my wrists and practising thrusts with my dagger.

At dawn, all the people gathered to watch. The Prince

of Syria, who had proclaimed the combat, had gathered together his own tribes and had even called the neighbouring tribes to attend.

When the strong man arrived, I drew myself up before him. All hearts were burning for me. Men and women, anxious for my victory, uttered cries saying: "Can there really be another champion strong enough to fight against this man who is so strong?"

Then my assailant took his shield, his lance and his armful of javelins, but I managed to ward off his missiles which fell to the ground. He used up all his arms without any result; then he leapt at me. At that moment, I shot off my bow at him and my arrow pierced his neck. He cried out, and fell on his face. I killed him with his own axe and, my foot on his back, uttered my cry of victory.

All the Asiatics shouted with joy. I made gestures of thanks to Menthu, the god of war whom we worship at Thebes. The Prince of Syria clasped me in his arms. I carried off all the victim's goods. I took his herds; I took everything that was in his tent; I enriched myself with his money. My heap of treasure grew and my herds multiplied.

Thus, then, had the gods shown themselves gracious towards me, who was reproached for having fled to a foreign country. So gracious were they that today my heart is filled with joy. I had been a fugitive, dying of hunger, a poor wretch leaving his country empty-handed, and now I have a good name at the Syrian Court. I give bread to the poor. I am a handsome figure in my clothes of fine linen. I own many serfs, my house is beautiful, and my lands vast.

Nevertheless, I was not at all satisfied. Now that old age

had come and weakness was laying hold of me, now that my eyes were heavy and my legs refused to obey me, and death was approaching, I wanted to see Egypt once more. "O god," I prayed, "who made me flee, allow me to see again the country where I was born and where I wish to die."

I sent a message to Pharaoh so that he might be favourably disposed towards me. His Majesty deigned to send me presents as valuable as those usually sent to princes of foreign countries and he wrote me the following letter:

"Order of the King to his servant, Sinuhi. Take note of the King's command and know his will.

"You have traversed foreign countries, leaving Kadima and setting forth for Syria, and you have passed from one country to another, according to the dictates of your heart. Therefore, you can no longer take part in the council of the Ancients. Nevertheless, I bear you no ill will. The Queen, your mistress, is in the palace and is still at the height of her power, esteemed amongst the royal households of the land; her children live in the palace. You will enjoy the riches that they will shower upon you, and you will live upon their bounty.

"When you return to Egypt and see your dwelling, prostrate yourself to the ground before the Sublime Portal and join the Royal Friends as before; for now you grow old and think of the day of entombment and of the journey to eternal happiness.

"Soon you will be spending your nights among the embalming oils and sacred bandages. There will be a procession for you on the day of your interment. They will carry you in a golden case, your head painted blue, a canopy above you. Oxen will draw your hearse, singers will go before you, and others will dance for you at the entrance to your tomb.

"They will utter the sacred words for you. They will slaughter victims at the funeral stone, and your pyramid will be set up in the circle of royal princes. It is not right that you should die in a foreign country, nor that the Asiatics should take you to the tomb wrapped in a sheep-skin. When you return here you will forget the misfortunes which you have suffered."

When this order arrived, I was standing amongst the people of my tribe. As soon as it had been read to me, I prostrated myself to the earth as though before Pharaoh, I dragged myself in the dust, and I rubbed dust into my hair. I walked round my camp rejoicing, and saying: "How can such indulgence be accorded to me, whose heart took me to strange and barbarous countries? What a wonderful thing is this compassion which delivers me from death, for my master and king is going to allow me to end my days at his court!"

And this is the letter I wrote in reply to his command:

"The servant of the harem, Sinuhi says: 'O most high master of the Two Egypts, friend of Ra, favourite of Menthu, the lord of Thebes, may Amon the lord of Carnac, Ra, Horus, Hathor, Atum and the nine gods who accompany him, the royal Uraeus who encircles your head, Nut and all the gods of Egypt and the isles of the Very Green Land give life and strength to your nostrils! May they shower their bounty upon you, may they give you life everlasting! May you inspire fear in all the lands of the plain and of the mountains! May you subdue and possess all the lands that are lightened with the sun's radiance! This is the prayer of the servant for his master who delivers him from the tomb. Your servant's flight was not intentional; I did not plan it beforehand. I do not know what took me from my native land. It was like a dream, yet I really had nothing to fear. No one pursued me, no one tried to harm me, and yet my limbs trembled, my legs took flight, my heart guided me, and the god who wished me to flee drew me along.

'Since you ordain it, I, your servant, will give up the offices which I hold in this country. May Your Majesty follow your own desires, for it is you who give life and it is the will of the gods that you live forever.'"

When they came to fetch me, I celebrated with feasting in my land, and I put my affairs in order. My eldest son became the chief of my tribe and the owner of all my goods, my serfs, my herds, my plantations and my datepalms.

Then I followed the road to the south. When I arrived at the frontier post not far from the Delta, the Egyptian general who commanded the guard sent a message to the palace to announce me. His Majesty sent a director of the King's household and ships laden with presents for the Bedouin who had escorted me to that point. I then bade them all goodbye, calling each by name. I embarked on the boat, which then set sail, and finally I arrived at the King's city of Taitou, which is one of the most ancient of royal cities.

When the land was once more flooded with the light of dawn, ten men came to escort me to the palace. The royal children, who were waiting in the guard-room, came to meet me. The Friends of the King took me to Pharaoh's dwelling and to the Great Hall of Pillars. I found His Majesty on the high platform beneath the golden portal, and I threw myself on to the ground and fainted before him. His Divine Majesty deigned to address pleasant words to me, but I was suddenly enveloped in shadows, my soul departed, my limbs failed, my heart no longer beat in my breast, and I knew the difference between life and death.

His Majesty said to one of his friends: "Raise him up and let him speak to me." Then he continued, "Behold, you who return after traversing strange countries, after flying from hence. You are old, and you shall be properly entombed. It is no small matter to escape interment amongst the Barbarians. Try to speak when you are questioned."

I was terrified and I replied: "What did my master say? I am not at fault. It was the hand of Amon."

The fear which gripped me at that moment was as great as that which had sent me off on the fateful flight. "I stand before you," I stammered. "You are life itself. May Your Majesty do as he pleases."

The royal children filed past me and His Majesty said to the Queen: "Here is Sinuhi, who has come back with the manners of a peasant. He has become indistinguishable from a Bedouin."

She gave a loud shout of laughter in which the royal children joined. Then suddenly they took pity on me and said to His Majesty: "No, in truth, my master, he is not like a Bedouin."

His Majesty replied: "Assuredly he is, he does really look exactly like a Bedouin."

Then the royal children picked up their musical instruments and passed before the King, singing a hymn in his praise, which said: "May your two hands do only good, O King, you upon whom rests the diadem of the south and the diadem of the north, and whose forehead Uraeus encircles. You have kept your subjects from evil, for Ra is favourable to you, O master of the Two Countries."

And they even added some words in my favour: "Grant us, too, this signal favour that we ask for the Sheik Sinuhi, the Bedouin, who was born in the land of canals in the Delta! If he fled it was because of the fear that you inspired in him; for he who looks upon your face turns pale and the eye which gazes at you has fear."

His Majesty's rage was appeased by this song and he deigned to say to the royal children: "Let him no longer have fear. Go with him to the Royal Dwelling and show him the apartment he will occupy. Let him be placed amidst the people of the Royal Circle. Let him be again as in the past, a wise man among the wise men that surround me."

When I departed from the royal presence, the children took my hand and we returned to the great double portal, so that I could receive my endowment. They assigned me an apartment, with bathrooms that were beautifully decorated; its furnishings were from the palace, and draperies from the royal wardrobe, all delicately perfumed. Three or four times a day I was brought delicacies, meat, beer and bread from the palace.

Feeling entirely rejuvenated, I shaved myself, I combed my hair which I had allowed to grow, following the custom of the Egyptians when they were in a foreign country. I got rid of my uncouth clothing, and dressed myself in fine linen. I scented myself with choice perfumes. I slept in a bed. And now all I had to do was to forget the country of sand and olive oil.

But now it was time to think of my future home, the tomb I was going to inhabit for all eternity. They made me a pyramid in stone and set it up in the centre of the funeral pyramids. The King's own architect chose the ground, the King's own artist designed the decorations, and his chief sculptor carved them. The director of the works of the necropolis searched the whole Land of Egypt for a sarcophagus, for offering tables, coffers, statues of my counterpart in stone and in metal and all kinds of furnishings. Then they appointed the priests of the counterpart, those who must keep the tomb in order and officiate at all the ceremonies.

As for me, I added still further to the furnishings and made all arrangements inside the pyramid and then I gave some lands near the city so that the profits would be used for the upkeep of my tomb and for the feeding of my counterpart, so that he should live happily in eternity.

Everything was magnificently finished. His Majesty himself decided to have my statue made. It was covered with gold and dressed in a scarlet robe, as befitted a friend of the Pharaoh. I was in the King's favour even to the day of my death.

*   *   *

This story has been told exactly as it was written in the book of Sinuhi and left in his tomb.

7
The Shipwrecked Captain

ARLY in the Twelfth Dynasty, about two thousand years before our own era, a captain was shipwrecked, and lost his ship, his crew and his goods. A sailor picked him up and took him as far as Elephantine, but all through the voyage, the poor captain was in despair because he was terrified that the Egyptian judges would hold him responsible for losing his ship.

Then, to comfort and reassure him, the sailor began to recount an adventure which had happened to him.

He began: "Let your heart be comforted, O captain mine, for here we are arrived in your country. The sailors have taken the mallet and driven the stake into the ground, and have slipped the mooring rope round it. They have given shouts of joy; and have thanked and worshipped the gods who protects boats. Each one, in his delight at having reached harbour safe and sound, has embraced his friend, whilst the crowd cries, 'Welcome to our shores!'

"It has been a wonderful expedition. We have not lost a single man. We reached the furthest extremities of the country of Ouaouart which is in Nubia, farther away even than the Second Cataract. We passed before Saumouit, an island opposite Philae near the First Cataract, and now here we are arrived back safely in our own country.

"Listen to me, O my prince, for I never exaggerate. You must wash yourself and pour water over your fingers; then you must appear before the King. You must speak to him frankly, reply when you are asked to speak, answer without losing countenance and watch your words carefully, for if a man's mouth is made so that he can defend himself it can also often be the cause of his downfall. Try to follow the impulses of your heart, and seek the words which will calm the anger of the King, so that he will set you free, guiltless and cleared of all blame.

"But so as to give you courage, I am going to tell you about a similar adventure that happened to me."

And this is the story he told: It was during the time when I had gone to the mines belonging to the King. I went by sea in the kind of ship which is no longer seen, much larger than those we use now. It was at least a hundred and fifty cubits long by forty cubits wide. You, who understand about boats, can imagine how great it was. There was a crew of at least a hundred and fifty, all first-class sailors, men from Egypt, who had seen the skies, who had seen the earth and whose hearts were stronger than lions.

They believed that the wind would not rise, and that we should escape disaster, but the gale broke just when we were in the open sea and before we reached land. The wind freshened and threw up a wave as high as a house. I tore up a plank and hung on to it. As for the boat, it disappeared and not a single one of the crew was saved. I, alone, thanks to my plank which floated and was caught up by a current, reached an island.

For three days, I remained alone without any companion save my own heart. At night, I slept in the hollow of a tree, crouching in the shade; all day I walked about trying to find something to put into my mouth.

I found grapes and magnificent leeks, berries in plenty, corn and melons to my heart's content, fish and birds. There was everything. I satisfied my hunger, scorning everything I did not fancy. I made myself some tinder and lit a fire, and I made sacrifice to the gods. And then suddenly, I heard a terrible noise, a voice of thunder, and I thought: "It is a wave of the sea!" The trees creaked, the earth trembled. I uncovered my face and I saw a huge serpent approaching me. Long!—oh as long as thirty cubits, with a tail of at least two cubits. Its body was encrusted with gold, its two eyebrows were of lapis lazuli, and it was even more handsome in profile than full face.

It opened wide its mouth and said to me as I lay flat on the ground before it: "Who brought you, who brought you here, you miserable wretch, who brought you here? Unless you tell me at once who brought you to this island, I will teach you what it is like to be invisible, for I shall reduce you to ashes."

"You speak to me and I do not understand what you say. I am before you like a fool without knowledge," I muttered in despair.

Then he took me in his mouth and carried me off to a

den, where he left me without doing me any harm. I was very much surprised to find myself safe and sound with all my limbs intact.

After he had opened his mouth to put me down, and while I remained on my stomach prostrated before him, this is what he said: "Who brought you here? Who brought you here, miserable wretch, who brought you to this island whose banks are washed by the waves?"

And, like a slave before his master, my hands outstretched in supplication, I told him of my shipwreck.

"Is it my fault, lord, if the wind and the waves washed me up here?"

Then the serpent softened his heart and said to me: "Have no fear, miserable wretch. If Amon-Ra has cast you up on my island, it is because he wishes you to survive."

"Listen to my prophecy. You will spend four months in my realm: then a ship will come from the country of Egypt with sailors whom you know. You will return with them to your own country and you will die in your own town. If you are brave, if you have courage, I promise you that you shall see your own house again, that you shall embrace your wife and your children, and that you will live among your brothers."

Then I stretched myself out on my stomach, I touched the earth before him. Prostrated thus, I cried: "You are kindly and you are mighty, O my lord. I will go and find Pharaoh and tell him of your splendour. I will have presents sent to you, presents of perfumes and ointments and the oil of sacrifice, which is the best of the seven oils offered to the gods. I will send you senna, incense of the temples, with which one is certain to gain the favour of the god. I will also recount what has happened to me and what I have seen, and they will worship you in my country, in the presence of the wisest men in the entire Land of Egypt.

"I will slaughter oxen in your honour and have them roasted. I will kill birds for you. I will have ships sent to you with all the treasures of Egypt, as is done for a god, for the friend of man in a far-away land which men know nothing about."

He laughed at me, he laughed at what I had said, and then he talked to me: "Do you not see here a great deal of myrrh growing? There is also plenty of incense, because I myself am the ruler of the country of Pount and I certainly do not lack myrrh. The perfume offered to the gods alone is lacking here in this island. But do you know what will happen? You will never see this island again, because, as soon as you are far away from it, it will be covered by the waves of the sea."

I lived for four months under the protection of the serpent. It was an enchanted island full of unimaginable treasures. There were seventy-five serpents who were the brothers and the children of the great serpent. There was also a young girl. As I was surprised to see her there, the great serpent told me how one day a star fell on to the island, all in flames, and that out of the flames came this beautiful young girl who was to be their companion.

And I sated my heart with all the marvellous stories he told me.

Time passed, the four months sped by and the ship appeared, as the serpent had foretold. Joyfully, I ran to the edge of the water, and climbed up into a high tree so that I could recognise those who were on board. They were sailors from my country.

I went off quickly to give the news to my friend the serpent, but I could see that he already knew, for he said to me: "Good luck, good luck, miserable wretch! Go to your dwelling, go to see your children, and I hope for your sake that you are well thought of in your town. Those are my wishes for you."

Then I lay down on my stomach, my hands outstretched, and he gave me presents—myrrh, perfumes worthy of the gods, pomades, senna, pepper, cypresses, all kinds of incense, hippopotamuses' tails, elephants' teeth, greyhounds, great monkeys with dog's heads as big as men, giraffes, and many more wonderful treasures.

I loaded all this on to the ship. Then I stretched out on my stomach, prostrating myself, and worshipped the serpent, who said to me: "In two months, you will reach your own country: you will take your children in your arms and later you will regain your youth in your tomb."

Then I went down to the bank where the ship was moored and I called out to the men on board. From the shore I gave homage and thanks to the master of the island, and the crew copied my gestures. We returned to the north, to the realm of the King. In the second month we reached the palace, as the serpent had said.

I went into the palace and in the presence of the King I told him what I had seen, and I offered him the presents which I had brought back from the Island of the Serpent. He was delighted with them and he complimented me before the wise men who surrounded him. Then he made me one of his attendants and gave me beautiful slaves in exchange for the presents which I had given him.

I managed to ward off his missiles

"Now, you see, O captain mine," added the sailor, urning towards his guest, "I have brought you back to he Land of Egypt. Profit by my example; go and find Pharaoh and tell him your story."

But the shipwrecked captain replied: "Make no mis- ake, my friend. It is in vain that you try to console a man who is already lost. Who bothers to give water to a goose the evening before it is to be slaughtered?"

For he thought sadly that he had not met the magic serpent nor had he brought back treasures from an en- chanted island to pacify the angry heart of his sovereign.

8

How Thoutiyi Took the Town of Joppa

N the days of the Pharaoh Manakpiriya, which was the first name of Thuthmosis III, who ruled over the Land of Egypt, there lived a general of the infantry called Thoutiyi, who had followed his master Pharaoh in all the expeditions to the Lands of the North and to the Lands of the South.

This Thoutiyi fought at the head of his troops. He knew all the stratagems employed in warfare, and almost every day he received as a reward the great golden rings which Pharaoh sent to the valiant, and which were called the golden reward of valour. He also received a large share of booty after each victory and many, many slaves, both male and female, for he was a very good infantry general, and had no rival in the entire Land of Egypt.

One day, a messenger came from Karon which is in Palestine between the river Jordan and the sea, and he was brought into the presence of Pharaoh, and His

Majesty said to him: "Who sent you to me? Why did they send you here?"

The messenger replied to Pharaoh: "It is the governor of the Lands of the North who sent me to you, saying: 'The vanquished of the city of Joppa has revolted against Your Majesty and has slaughtered your foot-soldiers and also attacked the chariots, and no one can hold out against him.'"

When the King, Thuthmosis III, heard these words from the mouth of the messenger, he became so furious that one might have thought him a leopard of the south. "Upon my life," he said, "by the favour of Ra, by the love which my brother, Amon, has for me, I will let him feel the weight of my arm." Immediately he summoned his noble friends, his officers and also his scribes versed in magic. Before them all, he repeated the message which had been sent to him by the governor of the Lands of the North. Then, with one accord, everyone was silent and no one knew what to reply for good or ill.

At that moment, Thoutiyi spoke up, and said to His Majesty: "Oh you to whom the entire Land of Egypt gives homage, order that I should be given the great staff which belongs to you, the staff called Tiout (for the Egyptians give names to everything and these objects also have a very real personality and existence). Order them to give me war chariots and some of the royal foot-soldiers chosen from the flower of the valiant men of Egypt. With all that, I will kill the vanquished of Joppa and I will take his city."

This advice found favour with Thuthmosis III, and he immediately gave the order to assemble the infantry and the war chariots as well as the ships which were to transport the army as far as the coast of Syria. And the great staff of Pharaoh was given to Thoutiyi as a sign of supreme command.

Many days passed at sea, but at last the coast of the region of Karon appeared, and the army disembarked near the city of Joppa.

Thoutiyi, who was versed in more than one kind of war strategy, ordered mysterious preparations to be made. First he commanded that several pelts should be sewn together to make a big sack, large enough to hold a man. Next, he had forged four iron rings of the kind used to handcuff prisoners, and two heavy chains, one to link the two handcuffs and one to link the two anklets. By his orders, also, the soldiers prepared strong ropes and heavy wooden collars, large enough to hold the neck of a man, heavy enough to weigh on them as the yoke weighs on the neck of an ox. To this great heap of "war-weapons", he added four hundred earthenware jars, each large enough to hide two crouching men.

When everything was completed, he sent a message to the vanquished of Joppa, saying: "I am Thoutiyi, the general in command of the infantry of the Land of Egypt, and I have followed His Majesty on all his marches to the Lands of the North and the Lands of the South, but the King, Thuthmosis III, became jealous of me because I was brave, and he wanted to kill me. I managed to escape well out of his reach and I have brought with me his great Staff of Office, the staff of Pharaoh, which I have hidden in the sack where my horses' hay is piled up. If you wish it, I will give it to you and I will be your friend, and with me you will be served by all the men who have followed me, the flower of the bravest in the army of Egypt."

The vanquished of Joppa let himself be persuaded by these fine words. Furthermore, he rejoiced exceedingly at the sound of them, for he knew that Thoutiyi was a brave warrior without a match in the Land of Egypt.

So he, in his turn, sent a message to Thoutiyi saying: "Come and join me and I will be like a brother to you and I will give you lands chosen from the richest in Joppa."

The vanquished of Joppa left the town escorted by his equerry and followed by women and children of the city and he came before Thoutiyi. He took him by the hand and he embraced him. Then he had him brought into his camp, but he did not permit Thoutiyi's companions nor the horses to enter. He broke bread with Thoutiyi, and they ate and drank together. Then the vanquished of Joppa asked: "What about the great staff of King Thuthmosis III?"

Now, Thoutiyi, before entering the camp of the vanquished of Joppa, had taken the great staff of Pharaoh and hidden it in the sack which held the horses' fodder, right in the middle of the hay. Then he replaced the sacks as before on the wagons, which had come from Egypt. While the vanquished of Joppa was drinking and talking with Thoutiyi, the men who had accompanied him were chattering with the foot-soldiers of Pharaoh and all were drinking together. Having passed an hour in drinking, Thoutiyi said to the vanquished of Joppa: "If it pleases you, whilst I remain here among the women and children of the city, let my companions bring in their horses and give them their food."

The men were brought in. The horses were hobbled, and the men set about feeding them. As they were undoing the sacks, they found the great staff of Pharaoh and went to tell Thoutiyi. Then the vanquished of Joppa said to Thoutiyi: "I wish above everything to see the Great Staff of Pharaoh, which they call Tiout. Since this miraculous staff is in your baggage, bring it here and let me see it."

Thoutiyi did as the other asked him. He brought the staff of Pharaoh to show him. He seized the vanquished of Joppa by his robe, and drew himself up to his full height, saying: "Gaze upon this, O vanquished of Joppa; this the great staff of Pharaoh, King Thuthmosis III, the redoubtable lion, the son of Sokhit the lioness-goddess, to whom the god Amon gives his power and his might!" And, raising his hand which held the staff, he struck the vanquished of Joppa a great blow on the temple, so that he fell unconscious at his feet.

Then Thoutiyi called his followers and ordered them to bring the handcuffs and the chains which he had prepared. Hands and feet securely chained, the vanquished of Joppa was put into the great skin sack. Thoutiyi then had the four hundred jars brought to him. He ordered two soldiers to climb into each of a hundred of them, until two hundred of his men were thus packed and hidden. That left three hundred jars which were filled with the ropes and wooden collars like heavy yokes. Everything was arranged so that the four hundred jars were alike and each one as heavy as the other. They were then sealed with the seal of Thoutiyi and each was loaded on to the back of a strong man. There were four hundred porters in all, and a hundred others were sent with them to serve as guides.

And this is what Thoutiyi ordered them to do:

"When you enter into the city you will open the jars where your companions are hidden. Together you will seize the inhabitants who are in the town and you will bind them with the ropes."

All these preparations had been speedily and secretly executed and, when they were completed, the equerry of the vanquished of Joppa was called so that he could be told: "Go quickly to your queen who has stayed in the town and tell her that your master is happy. For our kindly god has delivered Thoutiyi and all his followers to us. See, they have packed the booty taken from them in all these jars which are full and very heavy."

The equerry went at the head of the column to go and take the good tidings to his queen and he cried out: "We are masters of Thoutiyi!"

The gates of the town were opened to allow the porters carrying the jars to enter; as soon as they had passed through, they opened up the jars where their companions were hidden. Together they flung themselves upon the people of the town, large and small; they imprisoned them by the neck in the wooden collars and bound them with the cords from the jars.

When the army of Pharaoh had taken possession of the town, Thoutiyi rested and speedily sent a messenger to Egypt to announce the news to the King his master: "Rejoice; the god Amon, your father and your protector, has allowed the vanquished of Joppa to fall into our hands, as well as all his subjects and his city. Let some of your soldiers come out and join us to help lead in the captives, so that you may fill the house of your father, Amon-Ra, the king of the gods, with slaves and servants who will be under your sway from this time forth and for ever."

9

Satni's Adventure
with the Mummies

T was many years ago that a king named Ousinares had a son called Satni, who had a foster-brother called Inaros. Satni was very clever and well versed in everything. He spent his time in the Necropolis of Memphis reading there the books in sacred writing and the books of the Double House of Life, that is to say the magic books which tell of the life here below and in the Other World. He also deciphered the formulae which were written on the stelae, or stone slabs, and on the walls of the temples. He knew the virtues of amulets and talismans, and he also knew how they were made; and he was skilled in rewriting the powerful formulae, for he was a magician without equal in the entire Land of Egypt.

Now, one day, while he was strolling in the forecourt of the Temple of Ptah, carefully reading the inscriptions engraved on the walls, another man of noble bearing who was walking there began to laugh at what he was doing. Satni, incensed, said to him: "Why do you mock me?"

The noble person said: "I am not mocking you, but how can I help laughing when I see you wasting your time deciphering powerless formulae? If you really want to know of a masterly spell, come with me. I can take you to the place where there is a book which Thoth himself has written with his own hand, which will place you only just below the gods and very much above men. Two formulae are written there! If you recite the first, you can charm the earth and the sky, the world of the night, the mountains and the oceans; you will understand the talk of the birds of the sky and of the reptiles of the earth; you will even see the fish, for a divine force will bring them to the surface of the water. If you utter the second formula, even should you be already in the tomb, you would take on again the form you had upon earth and become alive again; you would see the sun rising in the sky with its circle of gods and the moon in the shape it has when it appears in the heavens."

Satni said: "By my life! You have only to name anything you wish for and I will give it to you, if you will take me to this place where this book is to be found."

The noble person replied to Satni: "This book is not mine. It has been put in the middle of the Necropolis in the tomb of Nenoferkephtah, the son of King Merenephtis. Be very careful not to take it away, for he will make you bring it back, a pitchfork in your hand, a lighted brazier on your head."

On hearing these words, Satni's head was filled with covetous desires, and he did not know whether he was on his head or his heels! He set off swiftly to see the King to whom he repeated the words he had just heard. The King said, "What is it you want?"

Satni replied: "Allow me to descend into the tomb of King Nenoferkephtah, son of King Merenephtis. I will take Inaros, my foster-brother, with me and I will bring back the book."

So Satni went to the Necropolis of Memphis with Inaros, his foster-brother. They spent three days and three nights searching among the tombs of the Necropolis of Memphis, reading the inscriptions on the stones and deciphering the formulae carved on the doors of the tombs. At last, on the third day, he found the place where Nenofer lay. When he had made certain that it was, indeed, his tomb, Satni uttered a magic formula. A hole opened in the earth and Satni was able to descend into the place where the mysterious book was kept. And this is what he saw, for in the darkness of the tomb, it was as light as though in full sunshine, because the radiance coming from the book lit up the surroundings.

Nenoferkephtah was not alone in his tomb, for his wife, Ahouri, and his son, Mihet, were beside him, or rather, their counterparts were with him, drawn there by the magical power of the Book of Thoth. Their bodies both lay interred at Coptos. Now this whole story was the result of Nenofer's desiring that Satni should undertake to bring mummies of his wife and son from Coptos, where they were entombed, to Memphis to be placed by his side, so that all three should be together for all eternity.

When Satni penetrated into the tomb, the wife of Nenofer, or rather, her counterpart, rose up on her funeral couch and said to him: "Who are you?"

He replied: "I am Satni Khamois, son of King Ousinares; I have come to take the Book of Thoth which I see there lying between you and Nenofer. Give it to me, otherwise I shall take it by force."

Ahouri entreated him: "I beseech you not to be angry, but to listen rather to the tale of all the misfortunes which have happened to me because of this book which you ask me to give you. It is because of it that we have lost so much of the time that we should have spent on earth.

"My name is Ahouri. I am the daughter of King Merenephtis and he whom you see there beside me is my brother, Nenoferkephtah. When I was old enough to marry, I was taken before the King at the hour of the day when he went to the harem to spend some time with his family. I had been sumptuously dressed for the occasion and the King found me very beautiful and he said: 'I see that my daughter, Ahouri, is already grown up and it is time that she should marry. With whom shall we marry Ahouri, our daughter?'

"Now, I had always thought that, according to the customs of Egypt, I should marry my brother, Nenofer, whom I dearly loved. I told this to my mother. She then went to the King Merenephtis, saying to him: 'Ahouri, our daughter loves Nenofer, her brother. Let us marry them according to the ancient custom of the Pharaohs.' When the King heard these words, he said to my mother: 'You have had only two children and yet you wish to marry them to each other? Would it not be better to marry Ahouri to the son of a general and Nenofer to the daughter of another general?'

"She replied: 'You are trying to pick a quarrel with me. Even suppose that I do not have any more children after these two, is it not the custom to marry one to the other?'

"But the King was obstinate. 'I shall marry Nenofer to the daughter of another military commander and that may be a good thing for our family.'

"When the day arrived for the feasting and entertainments before Pharaoh, they came to fetch me and take me to the celebration. I was very much upset and I did not look my best. Now Pharaoh spoke thus to me: 'Is it not you who were foolish enough to send word to me that you wished to marry your elder brother Nenoferkephtah?'

"I replied to him anxiously and respectfully: 'Well, then, let them marry me with the son of a general and let them marry Nenofer with the daughter of a general and may that be a good thing for our family.' And I began to laugh.

"Pharaoh began to laugh, too, and he said to the Governor of the Royal Household: 'Let them conduct Ahouri to the house of Nenoferkephtah this very night, and see that she takes all kinds of splendid gifts with her.'

"And that very night they took me as wife to the house of Nenofer, and, in obedience to the orders of Pharaoh, the people of the Royal Household presented me with a dowry of gold and silver, and the heart of Pharaoh rejoiced greatly.

"Nenoferkephtah spent his days happily with me, for each of us loved the other. In time, I had a little child, the one who is there before you. When Pharaoh was told the good news, he chose from the most valuable possessions of the Royal Household beautiful gifts in gold and silver and fine linen. My child was given the name of

Mihet, and it was inscribed in the registers of the Double House of Life. There, the soothsayers, the magicians and the scribes drew up his horoscope and predicted the future of the newly-born. They chose for him the amulets which keep away misfortune, and all this was inscribed upon the stelae in the Double House of Life as is done for the Pharaohs.

"Many days passed after that. Nenoferkephtah seemed to be on earth for the sole purpose of walking in the Necropolis of Memphis, which is the dwelling-place of the dead, stopping at every step to decipher and read aloud the inscriptions engraved on the tombs of the Pharaohs, studying the stone slabs of the scribes of the Double House of the King, and re-reading as well the epitaphs which they bore; for he was extremely interested in everything that was written there.

"One day, there happened to be a procession in honour of the god Ptah, and Nenofer went into a temple to pray. While he was slowly walking behind the column, still deciphering the inscriptions engraved on the chapels of the gods, an old man went by and saw him and began to laugh. Nenofer, hurt by this, said to him: 'Why do you mock me?'

"The old man, who looked like a priest, replied: 'I am not mocking you at all, but can I help laughing when I see you busy deciphering inscriptions which have no value? If you really wish to know a powerful spell, come with me. I will take you to a place where the Book of Thoth is kept, the book the god wrote with his own hand. If you repeat the first of the two formulae, you can charm the sky, the earth, the world of the night, the mountains, the waters; you will understand what the birds of the sky say, even the reptiles, every living thing; you will see the fish in the depths, for a divine power will bring them to the surface of the water. And if you read the words of the second formula, even if you should already be in the tomb, you will take again the form which you had upon earth; you will see the sun rising into the sky with its circle of gods, and the moon in the form it has when it appears in the heavens.'

"Nenoferkephtah, completely dazed, said to the priest: 'By the life of the King! Tell me what you most desire and I will give it to you, if you will take me to the place where this book is kept.'

"And the priest replied to Nenofer: 'If you wish me to show you where the book is kept, you must give me a hundred talents of silver, each weighing eighteen pounds, for my sepulchre, and you will have made two coffins of wood made to fit inside each other as is done for the rich priests.'

"Nenofer lost no time in calling a page and ordering him to give the priest the hundred talents of silver, nor in seeing that the coffins were made immediately.

"Then the priest said to Nenofer: 'The book in question is to be found in the centre of the Sea of Coptos in an iron casket. The iron casket contains a casket of bronze, the casket of bronze contains a casket of ivory and ebony, the casket of ivory and ebony contains in its turn one of silver. The silver casket encloses a casket of gold and in this lies the book. And right around the coffer in which the book lies is coiled an immortal serpent and a further guard of serpents and scorpions and all sorts of reptiles which stretch out in a circle of more than twelve thousand cubits.'

"On hearing these words uttered by the priest, Nenofer was so astonished that he did not know where in the world he was. He left the temple and came to discuss with me all that had happened.

"'I shall go to Coptos,' he said. 'I shall bring back the books and then I promise you that I will never again leave the Lands of the North.'

"But as for me, I disputed the wisdom of this project. I criticised the priest saying: 'Let him beware of the wrath of Amon because of what he has said to Nenofer. He has started a quarrel, he has aroused dissension, and the goddess of Thebes will be hostile to our happiness.'

"I lifted up my hands in supplication to Nenofer and implored him not to go to Coptos, but he would not listen to me.

"He went before Pharaoh and he repeated all that the priest had told him, and Pharaoh said: 'What does your heart desire?'

"Nenofer replied, without hesitation: 'That I might have the great royal ship fully equipped. I will take with me my sister Ahouri, my sister and my wife, and Mihet her little child, and I will take them to the Land of the South; I will fetch this book and bring it back.'

"So Pharaoh gave permission for the ship to be equipped and we embarked and completed the journey to Coptos. Our arrival was announced to the priests of Isis at Coptos and to the superior of the priests of Isis, and they all came down to welcome Nenofer, and their wives came to greet me.

"We disembarked on the shore to go to the temple of Isis and Harpokrates. Then we were taken to a beautiful house filled with lovely objects. Nenofer sent for a bull and a goose and some wine; and he made an offering and poured out a libation to Isis and Harpokrates.

"Nenoferkephtah spent five days enjoying himself with the priests of Isis at Coptos, whilst their wives kept me company and spent happy days with me.

"On the morning of the sixth day, Nenofer sent for a large quantity of pure wax. He made a magic boat with it and filled it with oarsmen and sailors. Then he uttered an incantation over them and brought them to life, gave them breath, and set the vessel afloat. After that, he filled the royal ship with sand and, taking leave of me, he embarked, whilst I waited on the shores of the sea of Coptos saying to myself: 'I shall know what is happening to him.'

"Then Nenofer said to the oarsmen. 'Row, oarsmen, row me to the place where lies this book. You have only to follow the enchanted barge which I have set upon the water. It will show you the way.' And they rowed without stopping, night and day, and they reached the place in three days, guided by the enchanted boat. When the enchanted boat stopped, Nenofer stood up and threw some sand before him; and a trough was hollowed out of the water.

"Nenofer saw a swarming mass of serpents, of scorpions and all kinds of reptiles. They were the guardians keeping watch around the casket containing the enchanted book. He recognised the great Serpent of Eternity twined around the casket itself. Nenofer then uttered a spell over the mass of serpents and scorpions all twisting together, and it stilled them. He could then penetrate right down to the Serpent of Eternity coiled round the casket, and that he killed. But the serpent, being eternal, returned to life immediately and took up its position again.

"Nenofer then attacked the monster and killed it again, but the serpent came to life once more and coiled round the casket to protect it. A third time, Nenoferkephtah attacked the serpent, and this time he cut it into two pieces, and buried the two pieces in the sand. This time the serpent died and did not come to life again.

"Then Nenofer approached the casket and he saw that it was a coffer of iron. He opened it and found a casket of bronze. He opened the casket of bronze and found a casket of cinnamon wood. He opened this and found a casket of ivory and ebony. This casket of ivory and ebony covered another of silver. Once opened, the coffer of silver revealed one of gold. Nenofer lifted the lid of the golden casket and saw that the book was inside.

"He seized hold of the famous book and took it out of the golden casket. He unrolled it and read aloud the first formula that was written there. And behold, he could charm the sky, the earth, the world of the night, and the mountains and the oceans. He understood clearly all that the birds of the sky said and also the fish in the sea and the four-footed beasts in the mountains.

"Then he read aloud the second formula that was written in the book and he could see everything: the sun which was rising high into the heavens with his escort of gods, the moon as she was in the sky, the stars in their places. He saw also the fish in the depths, made visible by a power which depressed the water around them.

"Then Nenoferkephtah, book in hand, uttered an incantation over the river and the waters closed up, returning to their previous form. He embarked again and said to the oarsmen: 'Oarsmen, row me to the place where is Ahouri, my sister and my bride.'

"They rowed him night and day and after three days arrived at the place where I was, seated on the shore of the sea of Coptos. I was not eating or drinking, I was doing nothing at all. I remained motionless, as I waited like a person who had already passed over into the other world, and is already installed in the Blessed Abode.

"On seeing Nenofer, I said to him: 'By the life of the King, let me see this book for which we have suffered so much.'

"He put the book into my hand and I read aloud the first formula which was written. I enchanted the skies, the earth, the world of the night, the mountains and the waters: I understood clearly what the birds were saying, as well as the fish and the four-footed beasts. Then I read aloud the second formula that was written, and I saw the sun appear with its escort of gods. I saw the moon at its rising and all the stars of the sky in their places.

"I wanted to absorb these marvellous formulae, but as I did not know how to write, I had to rely on Nenofer, my brother and my husband, who was a skilful scribe and a very learned man. He sent for a piece of papyrus, and on it he carefully copied all the words that were in the book. Then he moistened the papyrus with beer and dissolved it all in water. When he was certain that it had melted, he drank, and in this way contained within himself all that was in the book. And then he did it all again for me.

"We returned to Coptos the same day to rest a little and amuse ourselves before the Temple of Isis, then we embarked and soon we arrived at a place to the north of Coptos.

"Now the god, Thoth, had heard of everything that had happened to Nenofer concerning this book, and Thoth lost no time in appearing before Ra to plead his case. This is what he said: 'Let it be known to you that the book by which I govern is in the possession of Nenoferkephtah, son of Merenephtis. He has penetrated into my dwelling, he has taken the coffer with my book of incantations. He has killed the serpent, my guardian, who used to watch over the casket.'

"Ra replied to him: 'He is at your mercy, he and everyone that belongs to him.' Ra sent down a divine power from the skies, so that Nenoferkephtah should not arrive safe and sound at Memphis, neither should anyone with him.

"At that exact hour and at that exact minute, Mihet, the little child, escaped from beneath the awning which sheltered the royal barge from the sun: he bounded towards the edge and fell over into the water and was drowned, whilst everyone on board gave cries of horror and despair. Nenofer ran out of his cabin, and recited a magic formula over the child. Immediately the little boy rose up to the surface of the water, drawn by a magic power. Nenofer then uttered another formula over him, the power of which made him recount all that had happened. There was no formula known to man, however, which could bring back to life a being whom Ra had condemned.

"We returned to Coptos with the body of the child, which was taken to the Blessed Abode. We saw to it that he was well cared for. He was embalmed like a grown person, and was put in a coffin with full ceremony in the cemetery of Coptos.

"Then Nenofer, my brother and my husband, said: 'Let us hasten to return before the King learns of all that has happened to us, so that his heart is not troubled about this matter.' We embarked and set off again and soon we were about a league to the north of Coptos, at the place where the child Mihet had fallen into the water. I came out from beneath the awning of the royal barge. I leaned over the side, fell into the water, and was drowned, whilst everyone on board uttered cries of distress and despair.

"When Nenofer was told, he at once came out from beneath the awning and recited a magic spell over me which brought my body to the surface, drawn by a magical power. A second spell made me relate what had happened, as well as reveal the accusation which Thoth had made before Ra.

"Nenofer returned to Coptos with me. He saw to it that my body was carefully tended. I was embalmed as befitted a person of my race and of my very high rank; and then I was laid in the tomb where the body of the little child Mihet had already been placed.

"Once again Nenofer embarked and left the shore. He lost no time in reaching the place, a league to the north of Coptos, where we had fallen into the water.

"He conversed with his heart saying: 'Would it not be better if I returned to Coptos to be near them? If I return to Memphis now, and Pharaoh should question me about his children, what should I answer? Could I say to him: "I took your daughter and your grandson with me on the voyage, I let them die and yet I return to Memphis alive!"'

"He sent for a piece of fine linen of royal quality and

from it made a magic bandage. Then, laying the book upon his breast, he bound it solidly in place. Then Nenofer came out from under the awning of the royal barge; he leaned forward and fell into the water, whilst everyone on board uttered a loud cry. He drowned and his soul departed. Then everyone exclaimed: 'What great sorrow! what mourning there will be! behold the great scribe, the wise man unequalled in the Land of Egypt has disappeared.'

"The royal ship completed its journey before anyone in the world knew where Nenoferkephtah was. When it arrived at Memphis, Pharaoh was informed and he came down to meet it. He was in mourning robes and the whole of the city of Memphis was in mourning, as were also the priests of Ptah, the High Priest of Ptah and all the people of Pharaoh's Court.

"And behold: they perceived Nenofer caught up on the oars of the royal barge, where the magical power of the book of Thoth had drawn him so that his body was not lost in the waters. They lifted up his body and saw the book bound to his chest. Then Pharaoh said: 'Let us take this book which is on his chest'.

"The people of the court of Pharaoh, the priests of Ptah and the High Priests of Ptah said to the King: 'Our great master—may your life last as long as the life of Ra! What will happen to us, what evil may befall us if we touch this sacred book? See what has happened to Nenoferkephtah, he who is an excellent scribe, a very wise man, yet not even all his learning and magic could protect him from disaster.'

"So the book was left fixed to the chest of Nenofer. Pharaoh had the body of his son taken to the Blessed

Abode, the place where the embalmers worked for six-teen days. A further thirty-five days was taken to dress the body in sumptuous garments. Then for seventy days, it was wrapped in a shroud, and was finally laid in its place of rest in the middle of the other tombs.

"I have told you about all the misfortunes which befell us because of this book which you ask me to give you. You have no right to it, for because of it our life upon earth was cut short."

Satni said: "Ahouri, give me that book which I see there between Nenoferkephtah and you, if not I shall take it by force."

Then Nenoferkephtah drew himself up on his couch: "Are you not Satni to whom this woman has retailed all these misfortunes? This book of which you speak, are you able to take possession of it by means of your power as a scribe versed in the secret sciences, or by virtue of your skill in pitting yourself against me? Let us fight it out between us, then."

Satni replied: "I accept the challenge. Let us have it out between us." So the attendants of the Realm of the Dead, the servants of the counterpart of Nenoferkephtah, brought the chequered board used by players for moving pawns with dogs' heads or jackals' heads. It was placed between them.

Nenofer won a game from Satni; by reciting a formula over him to enchant him. Placing the gaming-board upon him, he made him disappear up to his thighs in the earth. Then he won another round, but this time he made Satni disappear into the earth up to his ears!

After that, Satni attacked Nenofer with his fists. Then he called Inaros, his foster-brother, and said to him:

"Return to the earth immediately, go and tell Pharaoh all that has happened and bring me the talismans of my father Ptah, which are superior to those of Nenofer-kephtah who only possesses the inferior ones belonging to Thoth; bring me also all my books of magic."

Inaros obeyed; he ascended into the earth immediately, he recounted to Pharaoh all that had happened to Satni, and Pharaoh said: "Take him the talismans of Ptah, his father, also all his books of incantations."

Inaros went down again in haste to the tomb; he put the talismans on the body of Satni, who at that very moment freed himself from his imprisonment in the earth. Satni put his hand upon the book and took possession of it, and, when he ascended again from the tomb, the light which radiated from it lighted the way before him, whereas behind him everything was shrouded in darkness.

Ahouri wept behind him crying: "Glory to you, O darkness, Glory to you, O light. All of it has been taken, all that we had in our tomb."

And Nenofer said to Ahouri: "Do not torment yourself. I will return this book very soon—a pitchfork in my hand, a lighted brazier upon my head."

Then Satni came up out of the tomb and he closed the door behind him just as it had been before. He went to have an audience with Pharaoh, and he told Pharaoh all that had happened to him concerning the book.

Pharaoh said to Satni: "Behave like a wise man, put this book back in the tomb of Nenoferkephtah; if not, he will make you take it back, a pitchfork in your hand, a lighted brazier upon your head."

But Satni was no longer listening; he had only one

preoccupation in the world—to spread out the roll and read the magic book.

After that, it happened one day that Satni, walking in the court before the Temple of Ptah, saw a woman who was so beautiful that he wondered whether anywhere in the world there could be another woman so lovely. She was so marvellously beautiful that she could have been created only by magic and by the demons. But Satni, when he saw her, did not realise that she might be Ahouri come back upon earth to seduce him and to take back the precious manuscript. Satni did not notice the gold with which she was covered, nor the fifty-two servants who accompanied her. They were none other than the fifty-two pawns from the magic chessboard of Nenoferkephtah, which he had by magic transformed into servants to form an escort for his wife.

No, at the moment when he was gazing at her, Satni was completely dazzled and he did not know where upon earth he was. He only knew how to call the page who was following him and give him an order: "Lose no time in following that woman and finding out all about her."

The page hastened to obey and he quickly discovered the route followed by the woman. He called the servant who was walking behind her and questioned her saying: "Who, then, is this personage?"

She replied: "It is Thouboui, the daughter of the prophet of Bast, the lady of Ankhouta (the quarter of Memphis built on the hill). She is going now to say her prayers before Ptah, the great god."

When the page returned to Satni, he repeated these words exactly. Satni then said to the young man: "Go, then, and say this to the servant, 'Satni-Khamois, son of

Pharaoh Ousinares, has sent me to say to your mistress that if she will accept the offer to come to his harem he will give her ten pieces of gold. He has decided to make her his wife, and he will not hesitate to resort to violence if it is necessary. He will carry her off and take her to a secret place where no one in the world will be able to find her.'"

The young man went back to the place where he had found Thouboui. He spoke to the servant and repeated his master's words to her. She cried out as though it were an insult to say such things. Thouboui then turned round to face him and said to the page: "Stop talking to that girl; come here and tell me what you have to say."

The young man approached Thouboui and said to her: "You will receive ten pieces of gold if you will accept the invitation to enter the harem of Satni-Khamois, the son of Pharaoh Ousinares. He has decided to take you for his wife, and, if you resist, he will have to resort to violence and you will be carried off to a place so well hidden that no one in the world will find you."

Thouboui replied: "Go and say to Satni that I am not a slave. If he wishes to marry me, let him come and live in my house. All will be made ready for him so long as he does not treat me like a serf."

And the page, when he had returned to Satni, repeated her words and Satni said: "This is exactly as I should wish."

Then Satni sent for a boat and embarked in it and did not take long to reach Bubastis. He walked through the town towards the west and came upon a very tall house surrounded by a wall and with a garden to the north and a flight of steps in front. Satni made enquiries as to whom the house belonged to and he was told that it was the house of Thouboui.

Then Satni went into the enclosure, and while Thouboui was being told of his arrival, he marvelled as he gazed upon the two-storied pavilion built in the middle of the garden.

She came down at once and, taking Satni's hand, said to him: "By my life, it gives me great delight that you have journeyed as far as the house of Bubastis. Come up with me."

Satni ascended the steps of the house with Thouboui and found himself on the upper floor of the house in a great hall, sanded and powdered with blue, with sand mixed with powdered lapis lazuli and turquoise. There were many couches covered with fine royal linen and on a table were cups of gold. Slaves put scented wood on the fire which gave off a fragrance like that in Pharaoh's Palace, and Satni was happy when he looked upon Thouboui, for he had never seen her equal before.

The slave filled a golden cup with wine and put it into Satni's hand, whilst Thouboui said to him: "May it please you to refresh yourself." But Satni said: "It is not to drink your wine that I come, but to take you to live in my harem."

She replied: "I am no ordinary person. If you wish to marry me, I must have a contract. You must undertake to support me in the luxury in which I have always lived, and you must give me rights over all your possessions."

He replied, without any hesitation: "Let them bring the scribe."

Immediately, they went to fetch him and brought him to Satni. Satni ordered him to make a legal document in

Thouboui's favour ensuring her status and giving her rights over all his belongings.

Thouboui thus became the wife of Satni, according to Egyptian custom. And shortly afterwards Satni was told that his children were below, so he ordered them to be brought to him. But Thouboui stood up, erect in her robe of fine transparent linen, and she said to Satni: "I am not a slave. You must sign a contract with your children so that later on they do not dispute your will with my children."

Satni then made his children sign the contract.

Then, later again, Thouboui went on: "I am not a slave; You must kill your children so that later on they do not dispute your estate with my children." Satni replied: "Let the crime conceived by your heart be carried out."

She had all the children of Satni murdered before his eyes, and then had the corpses thrown from the windows, and the dogs and cats ate the bodies. At that moment, Satni stretched forth his hand towards her, and at his touch she opened her mouth wide and let out a piercing cry. Satni swooned.

When he regained consciousness, he was in a furnace room, lying on the ground, stripped of all his garments. After more than an hour had passed, he saw a man, larger than any human being, standing on a dais surrounded by a great number of people, who were prostrate at his feet. He had the appearance of a Pharaoh. Satni made a movement to rise, but he held back ashamed that he had no clothes upon his back. Pharaoh then spoke and said to Satni: "Satni, you seem to be in a strange situation. What does all this mean?"

And the other replied: "I think that it must be Neno-ferkephtah who has put me in this pitiful condition."

Then Pharaoh went on: "Go to Memphis. Your children wish to see you; they are in the act of pleading with Pharaoh on your behalf. And Satni replied—"My great master, how can I go as far as Memphis? I have no clothes upon my back."

Then Pharaoh called a page and ordered him to bring a robe for Satni and he repeated: "Satni, go to Memphis. Your children are still alive, they are asking Pharaoh for you."

Satni set off for Memphis where he found his children full of life and he joyfully embraced them.

The real Pharaoh then said to him: "Do you not think that you were drunk?" But Satni had realised that the whole adventure was brought about by the magic of Nenoferkephtah, and that Thouboui was none other than this latter's wife, Ahouri. He related the whole affair to Pharaoh, who replied: "Satni, I have already come to your aid once. I told you: 'They will kill you unless you take back the book to the place from which you stole it.' But you did not wish to listen to me! Now, you must decide to take the book back to Nenoferkephtah, and you will go with a pitchfork in your hand and a lighted brazier upon your head."

Satni, realising that he was beaten, set off, a pitchfork in his hand and a lighted brazier balanced upon his head. And he arrived at the tomb of Nenoferkephtah and descended below. Ahouri said to him: "You have come, Satni. It is Ptah, the great god, who has brought you here safe and sound."

And Nenoferkephtah began to laugh. "Just as I

thought," he said. Satni could see that the whole tomb was lighted up with the radiance of the sun, since he had returned with the magic book, for with this book he had brought back light into the tomb, the light which he took away when he stole the talisman.

Then the three of them talked together for a long time like friends.

Satni questioned them. "Nenoferkephtah, what do you require of me now? You have broken down my resistance. Do you demand that I should do penance before you and humble myself?"

Nenoferkephtah replied: "Satni, you already know that Ahouri, my wife, and Mihet, my son, are interred at Coptos. Here, by my side, I have only their counterparts, thanks to the skill of a clever scribe, who knew how to write in my tomb the necessary spell to evoke them. What I ask of you is that you should set off for Coptos and bring back their mummified bodies, so that we may be again united, and this time for ever."

Satni left the tomb and ascended into the daylight. He went to Pharaoh and told him what Nenoferkephtah had demanded. Then Pharaoh said: "Satni, you must go to Coptos and bring back the mummies of Ahouri and her child, Mihet."

Then Satni replied: "May I be given the great ship of Pharaoh fully manned?"

And he was given the great ship of Pharaoh fully manned. He embarked, and it did not take him very long to reach Coptos. His presence was announced to the priests of Isis. They came before him, and went down to the shore to welcome him with full ceremony. They then went to the temple of Isis and to the temple of Harpokrates.

He prepared a splendid sacrifice. He sent for a bull and geese and wine; he slaughtered the bull and the geese as a burnt offering. He poured out the wine in libation. And all this was in honour of Isis and Harpokrates.

Then he went to the necropolis of Coptos, escorted by the priests of Isis. He spent three days and three nights searching among the tombs, moving and turning over the stelae of the scribes of the Double House of Life, deciphering and reading the inscriptions aloud, but he could not find the chambers where lay Ahouri and her child, Mihet.

From his faraway tomb, Nenoferkephtah saw that the search was in vain and the tombs could not be found, so he appeared among them in the guise of a very old priest.

Satni saw him and said: "You look to me like a very ancient man. Do you perhaps know where the bodies of Ahouri and her child, Mihet, lie?"

The old man replied to Satni: "The father of the father of the father of my father told the father of my father that the tombs of Ahouri and her child, Mihet, were beneath the southern angle of the House Eternal of the priest.

Satni said to the old man: "Then the priest's house will have to be destroyed in order to reach them. It is a very serious thing to disturb the dead and its counterpart. Perhaps this priest is your enemy and has done you harm —perhaps that is why you try to make me destroy him after death and demolish his tomb?"

The old man lifted up his head: "Let me be guarded closely, then, when the tomb of the priest is destroyed and if the bodies of Ahouri and Mihet are not found beneath the southern angle, let them treat me as a criminal."

Satni had a watch kept upon the old man, but they found the chamber where lay the bodies of Ahouri and her child, exactly beneath the southern angle of the tomb of the priest. Then Satni had the mummies of these important personages taken to the royal ship; he had the demolished tomb rebuilt, and replaced the mummy and the counterpart of the priest where it had lain formerly.

And the old man disappeared after Nenoferkephtah had explained to Satni that it was, indeed, he who had appeared at Coptos to direct the search and find the funeral chamber of Ahouri, his wife, and Mihet, his son.

Satni embarked in his turn on the royal ship and returned by the way he had come. Arriving at Memphis with all his escort, he saw coming towards him the Pharaoh, whom they had warned of his presence. He had the two mummies carried to the tomb where Nenoferkephtah lay and he speedily sealed the lower chamber.

And Nenoferkephtah and his wife, Ahouri, and their little child, Mihet, were at last together again for all eternity, and filled with joy. Nenoferkephtah ceased his manifestations in the land of the living and all of them enjoyed celestial repose. But Satni regretted having been forced to put back the magic book, before learning all the marvellous and magical science which it contained.

10

The Story of Satni and His Son, Senosiris

T happened many years ago, as you already know, that a king named Ousinares had among his children a boy called Satni who was well versed in many things and a very excellent scribe. He spent his time between the two pans of ink, one red and one black, with a jar of water beside him. His reed brush in his hand, he covered the long strip of papyrus with hieroglyphics and magic signs, gripping the roll with his left hand, whilst he was working with his right. He was a greater expert than any man in the world in the arts at which the scribes of Egypt excelled, and there was no wise man to compare with him in the whole of the land.

He solved riddles, and knew where to find the answers to the conundrums which the rulers of that time sent to each other as a challenge. It so happened that one day the King of Ethiopia sent a messenger to Pharaoh, daring

Satni was happy when he looked upon Thouboui

him to swallow the whole of the ocean at one gulp. Poor Pharaoh was saved from embarrassment by Satni who declared that his father would certainly undertake to swallow the whole ocean, but only in the exact state in which it happened to be when the challenge was made. So the King of Ethiopia would have to find means of holding up the flow of all the rivers, which poured without ceasing into the Land that is Green. Needless to say, the King of Ethiopia retired shamefacedly, without insisting any further.

In spite of all his learning, and the successes which it procured him, Satni was unhappy, because he had no son. His wife, Mahi, was just as sad as he was and never ceased praying to the gods to give them a child. Now, one day, when she had been to visit the Temple of Ptah, she fell asleep with exhaustion during her prayer, and, while she slept, she heard in her dream a mysterious voice, which promised that very shortly her wish would be granted.

A little later, Satni also heard from the gods. A voice spoke to him in his sleep, saying: "Satni, a son will be born to you very shortly. You will call him Senosiris and many will be the miracles which he will perform throughout the Land of Egypt."

When Satni awoke from his dream, after hearing these things, his heart was very glad.

And, at last, the day came when Mahi brought a son into the world, and when Satni saw the boy he named him Senosiris as he had been told. Mahi nursed the child carefully, and took great care of it. When the little child was a year old, he seemed to be two years old, when he was two, he seemed to be three, because he was so tall and his limbs were so strong. Satni could not let even one hour pass without seeing his child, Senosiris, so great was his love for his son.

When Senosiris was strong enough, he was sent to school, where very soon he knew more than the scribe who had been assigned to teach him. This small child, Senosiris, began to read and to decipher magic spells with the scribes of the House of the Life of the Temple of Ptah, who were the wisest of the wise, and everyone who heard him read the ancient and difficult texts, fluently, in a clear voice, were filled with astonishment. Satni took a delight in taking him before Pharaoh on feast days, so that the scribes and magicians at Pharaoh's court should make him talk and compete with them, for he always held his own with them all.

One day when Satni was washing on the terrace of his apartment, getting ready to go to the feast, and when the little boy, Senosiris, was also washing beside his father so as to go with him, Satni heard voices loudly intoning great lamentations and funereal chants. He looked outside from the top of the terrace, and perceived the funeral procession of a rich man, whose body was being taken to the tombs in the mountains, with all ceremonial honours and loud and lugubrious songs. He looked a second time below the terrace and saw the corpse of a poor man being borne beyond the city of Memphis, wrapped in matting, alone and with no mourners; for not one single man could be found to walk behind the body.

Satni cried out: "By the life of Osiris, the god of Amentit, all-powerful in the other world, may I be received into the realm of the dead like this rich man who is being taken with full ceremony, and not like this poor fellow, whom they are going to bury without any honours."

But Senosiris, his little son, said to him: "On the contrary, I would much sooner that you left this world like the poor man and not like the rich one."

These words very much surprised Satni and, deeply hurt, he said: "Is this really the voice of a son who loves his father that I have just heard?"

Senosiris replied: "If you would like it, I will show you how each of these people is faring, the poor man who goes unmourned and the rich man who is buried with so much honour."

Satni then asked: "And how are you going to be able to do this, my son, Senosiris?"

Then the small child, Senosiris, began to utter formulae unknown to Satni. He took his father by the hand and led him to a place in the mountains of Memphis, which he had never seen before. They passed between two high cliffs of rock by a passage which brought them to a great hall, then another, and another, and another. A vast crowd of people jostled and pushed forward in each of these chambers and no one tried to stop them.

On entering the fourth hall, Satni saw people who were running and moving about, whilst donkeys were eating on their backs. Others stretched out their arms to reach the baskets, containing water and bread, which were hanging above them; but the baskets remained out of reach, and other men hollowed out the ground beneath their feet to prevent them from drawing themselves up higher.

When they reached the fifth hall, Satni could see the venerable dead, who were well situated, but those who had been accused of committing crimes were standing pleading at the gate. The very pivot of the door itself was fixed to the right eye of a man who was crying out loud, praying and begging for pity. He must surely have been an enemy of the gods, thought Satni, as he and his son passed over, trampling the man underfoot.

When they reached the sixth hall, Satni saw the gods who make up the tribunal which judges the dead on their arrival in Amentit. They stood each in his rightful place, whilst the ushers of Amentit called out the cases one by one.

Facing the door, Satni gazed upon Osiris, the great god, seated on his throne of gold, crowned with a diadem formed by the white head-dress of Upper Egypt and the two ostrich feathers ranged on either side. On the right of Osiris, Anubis, the great god, was seated, and on his left Thoth, the great god, and after them, to the left and to the right, the forty-two judges, the gods of the Court of Justice of Amentit.

Before the tribunal, right in the middle, were the scales on which good and evil actions were weighed. Thoth, the great god, fulfilled the role of scribe and secretary, writing on his tablets; Anubis spoke to the accused and questioned them. Those whose evil actions outweighed the good, he delivered to Amait, the devourer, the dog of the ruler of Amentit. She was there with her crocodile's head, her lion's mane, her hippopotamus's body, her sharp claws and her huge throat, crouching at the feet of the lord Osiris, ready to devour the guilty whom the judges handed over to her.

On the other hand, he whose virtues Thoth and Anubis considered to outweigh his faults, was taken before the gods of the council who surrounded the master of Amentit, and his soul soared into heaven to live in joy among the blessed for all eternity.

Then Satni, marvelling at all that he saw in Amentit, perceived an attractive-looking man, dressed in fine linen, who was placed in an honourable position near Osiris. And Senosiris stood in front of his father and said: "My father, Satni, do you not see the important person dressed in splendid clothes and placed near the throne of Osiris? He is the poor man you saw being carried away from Memphis, without any funeral honours, and rolled up in matting. It is he. He has been brought into the Other World, into Amentit. His misdeeds were weighed against his good actions, and his virtues weighed heavier than his faults. When Thoth made up his account, he found that he had never had sufficient good fortune during his lifetime. To restore the balance, the tribunal decided to give him the funeral vestments and trappings which were the property of the rich man, whom you saw being conducted to his grave with such pomp and ceremony. And this is why the poor man has been able to take his place amongst the most revered of the blessed spirits around the throne of Osiris.

"As for the rich man, he also has come into the Other World. His virtues and his faults have been weighed in the balance, and his faults were found to weigh more heavily than his virtues; so it was decreed that his account should be put in order. It was he whom you saw a moment ago, screaming out because the pivot of the gate of Amentit was fixed into his right eye and moved over it whenever the gate was opened or shut. . . . By the life of Osiris, the great god, master of the World of the

Dead, if I said to you upon the earth 'May you be treated as this poor man is treated, may you not be treated as the rich man', it was because I knew what was going to happen to the latter."

Satni then said: "Senosiris, my son, innumerable are the marvels I have witnessed in Amentit! May I know who are these people who rush about, whilst donkeys feed upon their backs? Who also are these others trying to reach the food hanging out of their grasp, whilst others scoop out the earth beneath their feet to stop them reaching it?"

"I tell you, my father Satni," replied Senosiris, "that these first people are those who, when upon the earth, were accursed of the gods. They are now working night and day to earn their living, but their wives, changed into donkeys, rob them of everything they earn and eat upon their backs. Those who stretch out their arms in vain to grasp the food are those whom the god punishes for being greedy upon earth. For those who have lived good lives upon earth are well treated in Amentit, but those who have lived evil lives are treated ill. These things which you have seen in the realm of the dead of Memphis have been established for ever and will never be changed."

When Senosiris had finished these explanations, he returned by the way he had come, taking his father by the hand.

And Satni marvelled at the conversation that his small son had had with him, and he said to himself, "He may well become one of the blessed and a servant of the god, and I shall follow him into the Other World saying, 'This is my son!' That should be sufficient recommendation to make me also one of the blessed."

Satni pronounced a pious formula as a gesture of humility before the gods and he remained deeply astonished at the things he had seen in Amentit. What amazed him more than anything was the learning and the power of his little son. He turned the memory of these adventures over and over in his mind without being able to understand them. A new exploit of Senosiris was soon going to reveal to him the fact that the boy, whom he thought to be his son, was none other than a mighty magician of former times, who had come back upon the earth to protect Egypt from the misfortunes that were threatening her.

This is how it all came about: One day, when Pharaoh Ousinares was seated in the Audience Court of his palace at Memphis and when the Princes, the army chiefs, the great lords and officials of Egypt were standing up before him each according to his rank, His Majesty was told, "One of those Ethiopian pests has just arrived at the palace. He claims that he has a sealed letter on him." On the command of Pharaoh the man was brought before him.

He gave greetings and said: "Is there anyone present able to read this letter, which I bring to Egypt before Pharaoh, without touching the seal or breaking it? If there is no such scribe, no wise man of Egypt able to read the letter without opening it, I shall, on regaining my country, proclaim the inferiority of the Egyptians."

When Pharaoh and the Princes heard these words, they were beside themselves, and they cried out: "By the life of Ptah, the great god, is there any scribe learned enough or magician cunning enough, however clever he may be at deciphering hieroglyphics and mysterious writings that he can see, who can read a letter without seeing it and without opening it?"

Pharaoh then had an idea and commanded that his son, Satni, should be called. He was fetched in an instant. He bowed to the ground, prostrated himself and then stood up respectfully before Pharaoh, who said to him: "My son, Satni, have you heard what this pest of an Ethiopian has said to me? 'Is there in Egypt a good scribe or learned man who can read the letter which is in my hand without breaking the seal, and who knows what is written in it without opening it?'"

As soon as Satni heard these words he, too, was sorely perplexed. He replied: "My great lord, who can possibly read a letter without opening it? Nevertheless, give me ten days of respite so that I can see what I am able to do, so as to prevent these Ethiopians, these gum-eaters, from speaking of the inferiority of the Egyptians!"

Pharaoh then proclaimed "Your ten days shall be accorded to you, my son Satni!"

The stranger was given an apartment, and food was prepared, including shortcake according to the Ethiopian recipe. Then Pharaoh ended the audience and went to bed without eating or drinking.

Satni returned to his apartment, his head reeling. He rolled himself up tightly from head to foot in his robe, and then went to bed, still dumbfounded, and very much irritated at his helplessness.

When his wife, Mahi, was told about this, she came to find Satni and she passed her hands beneath his robe and said, "Satni has no fever, his limbs are lithe, his illness is a sadness of the heart."

He replied: "Leave me alone, sister Mahi! The problem which is troubling my mind is not a thing that it would be good to tell a woman!"

The little boy, Senosiris, then came in to him, and he leaned over Satni and said to him: "My father, Satni, why are you lying down with your mind distressed? Tell me of the anxieties that are locked in your heart so that I may dispel them for you."

Satni replied: "Leave me alone, my child Senosiris. You are far too young to be bothered with the anxieties which are disturbing me." Had he then forgotten his expedition into Amentit?

Senosiris insisted: "Tell them to me, so that I may calm your fears."

"My son," replied Satni, "it is a pest of an Ethiopian who has come to Egypt bringing with him a sealed letter, and crying out in challenge to us, 'Where is he who can read this letter without opening it? If no scribe or sage can be found in the whole Land of Egypt able to read it, I shall return to my country of Ethiopia proclaiming the inferiority of Egypt.'"

As soon as Senosiris heard these words, he burst out laughing, and, when Satni asked him why he was laughing, he replied: "I laugh to see you lying like this, your mind perplexed with such a small matter! Get up, my father Satni, for I will read this letter. I will decipher what is written without breaking the seal."

On hearing these words, Satni leapt up and asked his son: "Who can prove the truth of what you say, my son Senosiris?" Senosiris replied without hesitation: "My father, Satni, go into the ground-floor rooms of your apartment, and choose any book you like from the earthenware chest where they are kept, and I will tell you what book it is; I will read it without looking at it, standing before you with my back turned."

Satni got up, restored to cheerfulness, and Senosiris did exactly as he had promised. He read all the books his father indicated without opening them and without seeing them. Satni returned to his rooms on the ground floor, the happiest person in the world.

He lost no time in going to see Pharaoh to tell him all that the child, Senosiris, had said, and the heart of Pharaoh rejoiced. Freed from anxiety, he spent the rest of the day in drinking and entertainment. When the next day came, Pharaoh went into the Audience Hall, surrounded by his noble counsellors, he sent for the pest of an Ethiopian and had him brought into the hall, where he stood with the sealed letter hidden in his robes.

The child, Senosiris, stood close to him, and spoke up without waiting. "Evil be upon you, Ethiopian. You, the enemy, who angers Amon the great god! You dare to come into Egypt, the peaceful orchard of Osiris, the dwelling of Ra! You dare to defy us, saying: 'I will return to my land, proclaiming the inferiority of Egypt'. May the anger of Amon fall upon you! Before Pharaoh, your sovereign, I am going to recite all the words which are written in the letter you are hiding. Take great care that you do not say anything about them which is not true."

Senosiris spoke with such authority that the wretched Ethiopian prostrated himself before him, promising not to speak a single word that was not the truth. Then, before Pharaoh, before the Princes, the priests and the assembled chiefs, before all the Egyptian people who had gathered to hear him, Senosiris recited the contents of the letter without leaving out a word.

It was a very curious story that was recounted in this letter, a story of what had happened in the ancient days of the Pharaoh Siamanou, which had long been forgotten. Even at that time, the Ethiopians hated the Egyptians and did everything they could to make them look ridiculous and do them harm.

The letter told how three magicians of Ethiopia met together one day to work out ways of troubling the Egyptians. The first claimed that he could make spells which would cast Egypt into darkness for three whole days and three whole nights, so that no glint of light would be visible anywhere. The second claimed that he could cast a spell over Egypt which would make her lands barren for three whole years. The third, whose name was Nasi, claimed in his turn that, within the short space of six hours, he would bring the Pharaoh to Ethiopia, have him publicly beaten in front of all the people, and return him humiliated to his own country. And it was this last idea which appealed most to the King of Ethiopia. The story went on to relate how Nasi cast his spells, how the magic voyage took place and how the Egyptians who, of course, knew nothing of this sorcerer's tricks, were deeply distressed and horrified to find that their King had been beaten by magic during the night.

The King and his court and his counsellors anxiously talked together to try to find a way of avenging this shameful act. Among them was Panishi, the chief of the secret books, who swore that he would find a way to punish the Ethiopians. Calling upon Thoth, the accomplice of magicians, he first cast a strong spell to protect the King from being carried off again that night. He then sent sorcerers to Ethiopia to bring back the Ethiopian

King and beat him in public before the people of Egypt.
The King of Ethiopia appealed to Nasi to protect him,
and Nasi offered to go himself to the Egyptian court to
challenge his rival, Panishi. So Nasi, the pest from
Ethiopia, arrived at the court of Pharaoh and challenged
Panishi to meet him. Whereupon Panishi accepted the
challenge saying: "Be on your guard, for it is I who
challenge *you*."

Then the pest from Ethiopia, uttered one of his formu-
lae and a flame flared up in the Audience Hall, so that
Pharaoh and his friends cried out to Panishi in alarm,
"Come and save us!"

Panishi in his turn uttered the words of a spell and a
flood of water appeared from the south, and put out the
flame in an instant.

The Ethiopian called forth a great cloud of mist which
filled the Audience Hall, so thick that no one could see his
neighbour; but Panishi called up a great wind which dis-
persed it.

Nasi tried again: he called forth a great vault of stone
which rose up over and around Pharaoh and his court.
Pharaoh, looking up, saw this mass of stone and gave a
great cry of dismay, and the court also cried out in horror
at being thus imprisoned.

Now it was Panishi's turn to recite a formula. He made
a boat of papyrus appear, pulled down the vault of stone,
and loaded it into the magic vessel, which bore it right
out into the great waters of Egypt, as far as the lake of
Moeris.

Nasi had to admit defeat. To escape vengeance, he
made himself invisible, but Panishi soon brought him
back in the form of an ugly gosling, lying flat on its back

on the ground, with a hunter standing over it ready for the kill.

Forgetting all his pride, Nasi now pleaded for mercy, saying: "Forgive my crimes, give me a boat in which to leave Egypt, and I will go back to my country." But before doing this, Panishi made him swear never to return. And Nasi swore: "I will not come back to Egypt for fifteen hundred years." Then Panishi set him free and gave him a boat in which to return to the land of Ethiopia.

Now this was the story which Senosiris declaimed, and the Ethiopian fell at his feet in the dust, and had to admit that Senosiris had read correctly what was written in the letter.

Then Senosiris addressed Pharaoh, saying: "This man whom you see so confounded, O King, is none other than the Nasi in the story, who, now that the fifteen hundred years are up, returns to torment us. And by the life of Osiris the great god, master of the Other World, before whom I shall rest, I am Panishi.

"When I saw in Amentit, where dwell the dead, that this enemy, this Ethiopian, was going to torment Egypt with his evil-doing, I implored Osiris to allow me to appear once more upon earth, so that I could prevent him from declaring the inferiority of Egypt.

"Osiris exorcised me, and I came back to earth as the son of Satni, so that by my spells I might defeat this pest of an Ethiopian."

So saying, he wrapped himself in a great flame which

consumed him, there right in the middle of the Audience Chamber, before Pharaoh and all his friends and all the people of Egypt, and, in his turn, he disappeared like a shadow, and no one ever saw him again.

I I

The Doomed Prince

T was many years ago that a certain King of Egypt was perpetually sad, because he had no son to inherit the kingdom. He was so anxious for a son that he implored the gods of those times to send him one. They decreed that he should have what he so ardently desired, and, at last, one happy day, his wife gave him the long-wished-for son.

As with all Egyptian children, goddesses presided at his birth, the seven Hathors, young and beautiful, with rosy cheeks and heifers' ears. The Hathors were always gracious and smiling, whether they promised the newly-born happiness or sorrow, whether they enriched the child with gifts or saddened it with prophecies of misfortune. On this occasion, they gathered round the little Prince to predict his future, and they pronounced thus: "He is born upon an evil day, a bad, bad, bad day. He will be eaten by the crocodile, and if he should not die by the crocodile, the serpent will cause his death, and if neither the crocodile nor the serpent cause his death, it will be the dog."

When the people who were there heard these words of bad omen, they swiftly went to tell Her Majesty the Queen, who was naturally sad at heart. She straightway decided to take every possible precaution to prevent her beloved little boy from meeting such a terrible end.

Then Her Majesty had a house of stone built on the mountain top, and filled it with all kinds of furnishings and provisions brought from the King's house. A whole garrison was installed there to watch over the child, who was never allowed to go out.

When he was a little older he was allowed on to the roof of the house, which was built as a terrace, for Egyptian houses always have flat roofs. From there, he could see many things and he saw a greyhound, which was walking behind a man. He said to the page who was with him: "What is that animal behind the man, who is walking along the road?"

The page replied: "That is a greyhound."

And the King's child commanded the page to bring him one exactly like it.

The page went at once to repeat these words to His Majesty, who agreed at once that the Prince should have a young coursing-dog, "to keep his heart from sadness". And so they brought him a greyhound.

After many days had passed, when the child grew in years and his limbs became strong, he sent a message to his father, saying: "Now, why should I live like an idler? Even though destiny has three unfortunate things in store for me, nevertheless I will try to avoid them and do as I like. I do not think that my fate can be changed."

He set off, with his greyhound at his side

His father and his mother listened to what he had to say and decided to let him have his way. They gave him his greyhound, and a boat took him on a voyage to the coast of Syria, where he disembarked. Then they said to him: "Now then, go wherever you wish."

He set off, with his greyhound at his side. He went wherever his desire took him, and he lived on the game he hunted.

Now this country belonged to the Prince of Syria who had no son, only a daughter. And the Prince, who was unhappy to have no male heir, had a house built with seventy windows raised more than seventy cubits above the ground. After which, he had all the sons of the Princes of Kharon (which is Palestine) brought before him and he said to them: "Behold, he who reaches my daughter's window shall have her for his wife."

Now it was some time after these happenings that the Prince of Egypt arrived at this place when out hunting. He was welcomed by the Princes of the land of Kharon, who took him into their house, bathed him and fed his horses. They did everything in their power to please the Prince and to make him welcome. They covered him with perfumes, they rubbed his feet with ointments, they invited him to eat with them and they gave him their bread.

They began to make conversation with him out of politeness, and, in the course of conversation, they said to him: "Where do you come from, O good young man?" And he replied to them: "I am the son of a soldier who commands the war chariots of the Land of Egypt. My mother is dead, my father has taken another wife. This woman has children of her own and she has begun to hate me. Well now, at last I have got away from her."

Filled with pity, the Princes took him in their arms and embraced him. After many more days had passed he said to them: "And you, what are you doing here?"

And they replied: "This is how we spend all our time. We try to soar into the air; for, whichever of us succeeds in reaching the window of the daughter of the Prince of Syria will be given her as a wife."

The Egyptian Prince then said to them: "If you wish it, I will make an incantation that will cast a spell over my legs and I also will go and fly with you." But the others set off to fly as they did each day, and the Egyptian Prince stood afar off so as to see better, and, as he watched, from the height of her window the face of the Princess turned towards him.

After a few more days had passed, the Egyptian Prince went to fly with the Princes of Kharon and he himself flew and reached the window of the daughter of the Prince of Syria. She smiled at him and folded him in her arms.

Quickly a messenger was sent to rejoice the heart of the Prince of Syria and tell him that a man had reached his daughter's window.

The Prince questioned the messenger, saying to him: "Who is he, this man who has been successful?" They answered him, saying: "The son of a soldier who commands the war chariots, a fugitive from Egypt who has left his country to escape the hatred of his step-mother. She detests him because she has children of her own."

Then the Prince of Syria flew into a great rage. He cried: "Am I the man to give my daughter in marriage to a fugitive from the Land of Egypt? Let him return whence he came!"

And swiftly, swiftly they went to tell the Prince to go back to the place whence he came.

However, when the Princess heard this, she seized him by the arm and took an oath by Amon-Ra saying: "By the life of Phra-Harmakhis, if they take him from me, I will never eat again, I will never drink again. I shall die."

The messenger hastened to go and repeat these words to her father, who was furious and sent some soldiers to kill the young man whilst he was in the Princess's house. The Princess received them with ill grace and said to them: "By the life of Ptah, if you kill him, at sunset I, too, shall be dead. I will not spend another hour alive if I have to remain apart from him."

They retailed all this to her father, who was frightened by her threats. He had the young man and the Princess brought before him. The young man was seized with terror when he found himself before the Prince, but the latter took him in his arms and covered him with kisses, saying to him: "Tell me who you are, for as you know, you have become a son to me."

The young man replied: "I am the son of a Commander of the war chariots of the Land of Egypt. My mother died and my father took another wife. She began to hate me, so I fled far away from her."

The Prince of Syria gave him his daughter to be his wife. He gave him also a house, peasants and fields, as well as cattle and all kinds of good things.

After some time had gone by, the young man confided to his wife: "I know the future which awaits me. Three destinies threaten me; I shall perish by the crocodile, or by the serpent or by the dog."

The Princess replied: "Let us kill the dog which runs

before you." But he would have none of it. "Certainly not," he said. "I will not kill the dog which I have brought up from the time when he was quite small."

From this time onwards, the Princess never ceased to fear that harm might befall her husband. She was afraid, very, very much afraid, and would not let him go out alone. Now it happened that both she and her husband wanted to travel. They went towards the Land of Egypt, to walk there and to hunt across the countryside. And behold, the crocodile came up out of the river, which, of course, was the Nile, and it came right into the middle of the village where the Prince was staying. The Prince and his friends managed to seize the reptile, and imprisoned it in a shed, which was guarded by a giant. The giant never let the crocodile free. When it was sleeping, however, he used to take the opportunity to go out for a walk, always returning to the hut at dawn. This went on every day for twice thirty days.

Some time later, the Prince was resting one evening in his house. When night came, he lay down on his bed and sleep took hold of his limbs. His wife filled a jar with milk and placed it beside her. As he lay sleeping, behold, a serpent came out of its hole, and was about to attack the Prince. Luckily his wife was vigilant! She called the servants, and they offered the milk to the serpent. The serpent drank it and soon became intoxicated. It remained lying stretched out with its stomach in the air, and the Princess chopped it into pieces with an axe.

When the husband was wakened, he was filled with astonishment and the Princess said to him: "See, your god has allowed you to escape one of the destinies which threatened you. I am sure he will let you escape the others." The Prince immediately made offerings to the god, worshipping him and acclaiming his powers every day of his life.

When a further period of time had passed, the Prince went to stroll in the countryside around his own lands. And as he never went out alone, his dog trotted behind him. They arrived by the banks of the Nile. But whilst the dog was swimming, the crocodile came up out of the water and seized the Prince. Fortunately, he dragged him along on the side where the giant's house stood, and the latter came out just in time to save the Prince.

Then the crocodile spoke to the Prince, saying: "Ah, I am the destiny which is following you. Whatever you may do, you will always cross my path. The giant, you and I must always be meeting. The giant bothers me more than you do, so I am going to make a bargain with you. If you will kill the giant, I will let you go: but if you do not get rid of this giant, who keeps me prisoner here, it will be you who will go to your death. Think carefully and understand me. You had better swear to kill the giant; for, if you refuse, you will see death." And he waited for the answer.

When the earth was once again radiant with dawn, the dog arrived unexpectedly and saw that his master was in the power of the crocodile, who repeated once again: "Will you swear to kill the giant?"

The Prince answered him saying: "Why should I kill the one who has guarded me and who has prevented you from killing me outright?"

"Very well," said the crocodile, "Let destiny have its way! If by sunset you do not make me the oath which I demand, you will see death." The dog heard these words, and ran to the house, where he found the daughter of the Prince of Syria in tears, for her husband had not returned since the day before.

When she saw the dog returning alone, without his master whom he never left, she burst into sobs, she cried aloud and she beat her breast in despair. The dog, however, seized her by her dress and dragged her towards the door as though to ask her to go out. She got up and took the axe with which she had killed the serpent, and followed the dog to the place on the shore where the giant was. There she hid herself in the reeds and waited. She stayed there without eating or drinking, but all the time she never stopped praying to the gods on her husband's behalf.

When evening came, the crocodile spoke again: "Will you swear to kill the giant? If not, I will take you to the river and you will see death."

But the Prince kept firmly to his first reply: "Why should I kill the one who has looked after me?"

Then the crocodile seized him and carried him towards the river just at the place where the woman was concealed among the reeds. Suddenly she leapt out and, just as the crocodile opened wide its jaws, she struck it a blow with the axe. Meanwhile, the giant flung himself at the crocodile and despatched it.

Then the woman embraced the Prince and said to him: "You see, your god has allowed you to escape the second evil which threatened you; he will assuredly save you also from the third." And straightway the Prince offered presents to the god, vowing to worship him and exalt his power every day of his life.

After a further period of time had passed, enemy forces

penetrated into the country. The sons of the Prince of Kharon, furious that the Princess had married a man they took for an adventurer, had assembled their soldiers and their chariots. They had defeated and scattered the army of the Prince of Syria, and the Prince himself remained in their hands a prisoner. As they could not find the Princess and her husband anywhere, they asked the Princess's father: "Where is your daughter? Where is the son of the commander of the chariots of the Land of Egypt to whom you gave your daughter?"

The old Prince replied to them: "He has gone with her to hunt the beasts of the countryside. How should I know where they are?"

Then they deliberated and talked one with another, saying: "Let us break up into little groups and spread out over the entire world, and whosoever finds this couple must kill the young man and, as for the woman, he can do what he likes with her."

So they set off in little groups, some to the east, some to the west, some to the north and some to the south. And those who were moving towards the south arrived at the Land of Egypt, and even at the very town where the young man and the daughter of the Prince of Syria were staying. But the giant saw the arrival of the little group of newcomers and ran to the young man, crying: "Behold! Seven of the sons of the Prince of the country of Kharon are come here to find you. If they succeed they will kill you, and they will do what they like with your wife. There are too many of them for us to resist, so you must flee before them, and I will return to my brothers."

The young Prince called his wife. He took his dog with him, and together they went and hid in a cave in the mountains. They had been there for two days and two nights when the sons of the Prince of the land of Kharon arrived with their soldiers, and passed in front of the opening of the cave, without any of them seeing the Prince. Unfortunately, just as the last one was passing, the dog came out, ran after him and started barking.

Immediately the sons of the Prince of Kharon recognised him, for he was a greyhound of good strain, and they all retraced their steps to look into the cave. The woman threw herself in front of her husband to protect him, but a lance struck her and she fell dead at his feet.

The young man killed one of the Princes with his spear and the dog killed another, tearing him with its teeth, but the others struck him with their lances and he fell to the earth unconscious. The Princes dragged the bodies out of the cave, and left them lying on the ground, so that the wild beasts and the birds of prey might come and devour them. Then they set off to go and join their companions who had gone towards the east and the west and the north, and to return with them to their own region and share the lands of the Prince of Syria.

When the last of them had withdrawn, the young man opened his eyes and saw his wife stretched out dead on the ground. He saw also the body of his dog. Then he moved a little and he cried out in lamentation: "In truth it must be that the gods are inexorable in carrying out these decrees of fate. The Hathors decided at my birth that I should perish by a dog, and see how their prophecy has come to pass. For it was certainly the dog who delivered me to my enemies. I shall soon die, for without the two beings who lie there beside me, life is unendurable." Then he raised his hands to heaven and cried: "I have not sinned against you, O gods. That is why I beseech you to grant me an honourable burial in this world, and a just voice to bear witness for me before the judges of Amentit."

He fell down again as though dead. But the gods had heard his voice. Now the nine gods together came towards him. Then Ra-Harmakhis said to his companions: "Destiny has been accomplished. Now let us give a new life to these two wedded creatures, for it is right to reward such devotion."

The mother of the gods nodded her head to show approval of these words of Ra-Harmakhis, and she said: "Assuredly, such devotion deserves a very great reward."

The other gods said the same and then the seven Hathors came forward, chanting: "Destiny is fulfilled, now let them return to life." And they returned to life at that very moment.

In his delight at recovering his life with his wife and his dog, the Prince decided that from that time forth he would no longer hide his real identity. Accordingly he told his whole story to the Princess and they went to the palace where the Prince made himself known to the King, his father. The King was very happy to find him safe and sound, now protected from the misfortunes which had been predicted. Pharaoh did not forget to give his son a splendid army, infantry, cavalry and many chariots of war with which to go forth and punish his enemies.

The Prince set out with his army for the country of Syria, the country whence he had brought his wife. There he found the Princes who had pursued him and who, after having attacked him, had shared the belongings of the Prince, his father-in-law. He put them all to death; he re-established the Prince of Syria upon the throne, and then returned to Egypt, loaded with all the booty taken from his enemies. All the treasure which he brought back he gave as an offering to the god, Amon-Ra. After this he spent the rest of his days in happiness with his wife and his dog, never neglecting to worship Ra and exalt his power every single day of his life.

Everyone, however, does not tell this story in the same way. Some say that the gods themselves cannot change man's destiny once it is decreed, and that nothing could have saved the Prince from his fate. They affirm that the dog, in the fury of combat, had wounded his master by mistake, that the Prince died from his wound and that thus the prediction of the Hathors was fulfilled. But everyone agrees that the merciful gods reserved the happiest of lives in the Other World for the Prince and his wife.

12

The Story of the
Princess of Bakhtan

A T the time when King Rameses II reigned over Egypt and the neighbouring realms, far beyond the frontiers which formerly limited the territories of his ancestors, he decided one day to go on a voyage. He announced to the whole court and to all his friends that he was going to undertake a journey throughout his possessions.

He soon set out. His warships waited on the Red Sea to transport and escort him. Upon the highways of the land, the whole Egyptian army, the infantry, the cavalry and the chariots drawn by splendid war-horses, accompanied him to do him honour and to protect him from all danger.

The huge convoy moved along slowly. At each town Pharaoh made a halt of several days or several weeks. The chiefs and the Princes of the country hastened to meet him to pay their homage; to make gifts to him of all the rarest and best that they could produce; to live for a while with the pomp and magnificence which surrounded the sovereign, as well as to be present at the religious ceremonies in honour of Amon-Ra, the great god. And it even happened that chiefs as yet unknown to the King came humbly to make their submission, and to say to His Majesty: "We should like to serve Pharaoh."

And these princes did not forget to lay at the feet of the sovereign the tribute which was due to him, and their offerings surpassed all that might be expected. For the fame of Pharaoh was so great that, to gain his protection, they would have sacrificed all their treasures. Every day new wagons joined in the triumphal procession, loaded with gifts that were as numerous as they were splendid. Thus without striking a blow, and simply by reason of his prestige, and above all, thanks to the protection of Amon-Ra, the all-powerful, Pharaoh saw his empire increasing before his eyes, and the number of his subjects multiplying.

During this triumphal expedition, Pharaoh Rameses II saw again the battlefields where, in his youth, he had led the armies of Egypt to victory. He sojourned for some time in Kadesh in Syria, the place of the famous combats which he had waged against the Hittites. He ordered one of the scribes of his suite to read the official record of these glorious days, and he felt again the same emotions. After which, Pharaoh ordered sacrifices to be offered up, and chants to be sung, to thank once more the benevolent gods whose favourite he was.

Then he ordered the scribes to examine and restore the inscriptions carved on the stelae, which had been set up to perpetuate the memory of the great victories of the

Egyptians. Everywhere he had these inscriptions copied in the course of his triumphal progress, as far as the rocks of Beirut and Smyrna. And everywhere along the way, the peasants crowded forward to see him and greet him in festive clothing, after having poured fragrant oil over their hair. The townspeople stood up by their doorways, their arms full of flowers, garlands and green branches. And everywhere was filled with joy as Pharaoh approached.

All the Princes vied with each other in their homage. Each wanted to surpass all the others in the splendour and value of his gifts, so as to monopolise the goodwill and gratitude of the great Rameses.

Thus from celebration to celebration, the procession reached the Land of the Upper Euphrates, which belonged by right to the Prince of Bakhtan. This Prince welcomed His Majesty even more magnificently than the others had done. To his homage and his presents he added an excellent oration, composed by the most famous poets of his country, and full of the most flattering utterances. He besought the gods to favour Rameses with a long and happy life, and to grant him victories and prosperity. Not knowing what more he could add to make his welcome even greater than the preceding acts of homage, he terminated his speech by offering Pharaoh the most precious, the most beautiful of the treasures in his possession, the marvellously lovely Princess, his eldest daughter.

The Princess was indeed so beautiful, so very beautiful that Pharaoh himself was dazzled at the sight of her. He immediately promised that he would take her for his wife and that she should follow him to Egypt. In his delight, he even gave her a new name, an Egyptian name. He decided that from that time forth she should be called Neferu-Ra, and that she should be the most important of all the queens in his harem at Thebes.

Now when Pharaoh took her back to Egypt he did exactly as he had said. Neferu-Ra, although she was of foreign birth and although she was not descended from the line of Pharaohs which goes back to the god Osiris himself, was treated as the sovereign of the entire Land of Egypt, and the highest of them all, because she was the favourite among her husband's wives. He held her to be the most beautiful princess in the whole world, and he would, without hesitation, have overthrown the entire universe rather than that she should suffer the least inconvenience.

Now when the autumn of the fifteenth year of the reign of Pharaoh came, His Majesty was at Thebes, with all his court, to celebrate the great festivities in honour of Amon-Ra, the greatest of all the gods. It was in the temple of Luxor that the ritual ceremonies took place. Between the high pillars of the immense hall, where the splendid paintings were scarcely dry, all the friends of Pharaoh were gathered together. Behind them stood the officials of the court and the attendants of the sovereign, and behind these again the royal guard held back the crowd which surged forward to pass the enormous column. Pharaoh looked with pleasure and satisfaction at the beautiful frescoes in bright colours, which depicted his victorious campaigns, explained by long inscriptions. He admired the effigy of himself, huge, like a god who dominates humanity, standing in his chariot and driving his war horses. The artist had made him very much larger than the soldiers and the vanquished enemy, to denote his majesty.

The gates of the Hall of the Ship opened to let the procession pass out. Amon-Ra, carried in triumph by priests of his temple, was to follow the sacred way, lined by sphinxes, and then pass through the streets of the town on his way to the Nile. The entire population uttered shouts of joy.

Just then, the arrival of the ambassador of Pharaoh's father-in-law, the Prince of Bakhtan, was announced. He brought a message from his master, and the long file of porters who followed him announced many presents destined for Pharaoh and his royal bride, Neferu-Ra. The ambassador was immediately received by His Majesty in one of the inner courts of the Temple of Amon. He threw himself to the ground before the King, his face in the dust, and waited for the order to rise. Behind him, the porters pressed forward, loaded with cases carefully packed for the long, long journey from Bakhtan to Thebes. Each one placed his burden at the feet of the sovereign.

Then the envoy of the Prince of Bakhtan spoke.

He told Pharaoh how he came to him on behalf of his master, and expressed the latter's wishes for Pharaoh's health and prosperity. Then he came to the object of his journey which was to make an important request. "The sister of the revered queen, Neferu-Ra, who remained in her country of Bakhtan, she who bore the name of 'Daughter of Happiness', has fallen dangerously ill, and the doctors of Bakhtan—skilful though they be—know nothing about the malady. They all agree that they can no longer answer for her precious life. She is pale, listless and exhausted.

"The Prince of Bakhtan, my master, sends me to be seech Your Majesty to do something to save her. Withou doubt, if the doctors in Egypt, so much wiser and mor powerful than those of Bakhtan, would come to see her these men who understand all illnesses and have all the remedies would be able to cure her."

At this moment, the Queen Neferu-Ra, who was present and in despair, added her pleas to those of the Prince, her father; she threw herself at the feet of Pharaoh, imploring him to send swiftly to the country of Bakhtan the best doctors, to relieve and save her well-beloved sister, Daughter of Happiness.

Not wanting to refuse his wife, the Queen Neferu-Ra, anything, His Majesty immediately summoned a dozen or more of the best and most skilful of his own private doctors who were despatched without delay to the far-away realm of Bakhtan, and ordered to make all speed, on pain of death. And the King and the Queen, and all the court offered up prayers and sacrifices, hoping that the Princess, Daughter of Happiness, would recover her health and her life.

Three years later, Pharaoh saw the twelve doctors returning ashamed and pitiful. They had travelled as swiftly as possible; they had seen the sick Princess and had tried all the remedies they knew, but without any success. Nothing had been of any use, neither the fumigations of incense, nor those of fresh oil. They had made her eat the liver of a donkey without any result. She had swallowed a whole phial of castor-oil, and they had smeared her entire body with a special ointment, composed of twenty-seven elements, including lizard's blood, but she had remained motionless, pale and almost lifeless. Then they had tried other things. Ranged in a circle around her, they had chanted in the accepted tones, and repeated three times, the magic formula: "Depart from hence, O cold, son of cold, which breaks bones, crushes the head, and wounds the seven openings of the head."

The Princess, Daughter of Happiness, had half-opened her drooping eyelids and murmured: "They have not even noticed that I have not got a cold." The Prince of Bakhtan, furious, had then driven them out ignominiously, and had ordered them to return to Egypt, quickly, quickly. At the same time, the ambassador was sent to ask Pharaoh for more effective help.

Pharaoh, himself infuriated, sent for a court official and ordered that each of the doctors should receive a hundred strokes of the stick, the staff of Pharaoh, long and heavy, to cure the fatigues of their journey. And not one of them came back to complain.

Then Pharaoh summoned the whole court and all his friends and told them what the ambassador from the Prince of Bakhtan had said. Then the Queen Neferu-Ra began to weep and to bewail the sad condition of her well-beloved sister.

The friends of Pharaoh, the attendants and the soldiers of the army of Egypt all began to weep and wail, to discuss the bad news, to deplore the serious illness of the precious sister-in-law of the sovereign, and to swear to cure her.

But Pharaoh put a question to them: "Who is the most skilful and the most wise of the magicians attached to my court? For, since the most famous doctors of the entire Land of Egypt have been powerless to cure her, I think it would be best now to send to the country of Bakhtan a magician from the temple of Thoth."

The friends cried out with one voice: "That is true, O Majesty! If the twelve doctors whom you sent to your illustrious father-in-law were not able to cure the Princess, Daughter of Happiness, it is because they are not sufficiently wise. They are apprentices, small practitioners, good enough, perhaps, to care for the peasants. They must be replaced by a magician of the first order, an ancient sage, a scribe of your own household."

Then Pharaoh asked: "Which is the best?"

And all of them answered with one voice: "It is the scribe, Tehuti."

Then the scribe, Tehuti, was sent for without delay, and he was brought quickly before Pharaoh. Even more quickly, he was given the order to set off for the country of Bakhtan and to travel with all speed. Once arrived there, he was to do all in his power to deliver the unfortunate Princess from her troubles. With such a long journey in front of him, there was not a minute to lose, and Tehuti, the scribe, hastened to set forth, protected by the strict orders of Pharaoh. Everything along the way must be stopped to let him pass.

Tehuti, the scribe, well versed in the science of magic, made great haste.

Arriving in the country of Bakhtan, he was admitted to the presence of the Princess, and authorised to question her so that he could study the symptoms of her malady, and the pains which had afflicted her for so long.

He reflected at leisure. Then he took up his brush and his ink-pot, and began to trace some signs on papyrus. Slowly, with concentration, so as not to make a mistake, he wrote a powerful spell, known to very few living men, for it was one of the secret formulae of Thoth himself.

Then he dissolved the papyrus in a little beer, and asked the patient to swallow this drug, whilst he recited in a low voice another formula, even more powerful than the first, which he repeated seven times in succession, without a pause, and without taking breath.

The Princess made a wry face, because the beer mixed with papyrus and ink did not taste good, but that was the only result. Then the scribe, Tehuti, announced that he must take stronger measures, but, first of all, he must await a favourable day.

When this day arrived, he caused to be placed in all the corners of the palace, and in the room of the illustrious patient, great bunches of sacred herbs (which he had taken care to bring from Egypt, along with cases of medicinal plants and mysterious ingredients).

He dropped a packet of these herbs into the magic brew and twice a day, at sunrise and at sunset, he sprinkled the whole royal dwelling with it, chanting strange words, which no one understood.

When night came, he forbade the lighting of any torches. The room was illuminated by wicks soaked in oil of colza and in melted crow fat, poured into a bronze vessel. He asked the Princess to block her mouth, her ears and her nostrils with wads of cotton soaked in gum, after placing at her feet shoes cut from apple-wood. She had also to recite twenty-three times one of the psalms of Thoth, the wise god.

"Be calm, O pain, and be appeased by the power of him who, when he says to a thing, 'Be!' then it is so."

During this time the wise scribe lighted a brazier upon some charcoal of vine wood, and then threw on the fire some tablets of his own confection, large as chick peas and composed of myrrh and aloes, rue and rosemary.

A thick smoke enveloped the Princess, who tossed and turned at least a hundred times. The scribe, Tehuti, hoped that she would thus expel the demon which was causing her suffering and that the next day would find her relieved, rested and cured.

But the next day, she declared that she had had a nightmare and she was paler and weaker than ever.

The scribe, Tehuti, began to doubt his own learning. Nevertheless, he tried some other remedies.

He composed a new cure according to the most secret formulae which had been taught him in his youth by the very, very old priests of Thoth, which they had received from Thoth himself. He put into it some rosewater, the leg of a hoopoe, the feathers of a phoenix and the heart of a black cat.

He made the Princess drink this nauseating dose, after which he gave her a cup of oil, in which had been boiled an old book, until it had entirely disappeared. And the unfortunate Princess had to hold her nose before she could take in this magic beverage, saying to herself:

"Come, O cure, come to me.
Destroy the invisible things in my heart and limbs;
May the magic formula act powerfully as a remedy;
May the remedy be strong because of the magic formula."

But all this was in vain; there was no improvement in the condition of the patient.

Tehuti, the wise scribe, had to admit that all his learning, all his experience, all his wisdom and all his magic had failed.

He thought with terror that over there in Thebes in Egypt, the Queen Neferu-Ra was waiting for a message giving news of her sister's recovery, and he shivered at the thought of Pharaoh's anger, at the betrayal and the sorrow of his well-beloved spouse. Finally, he had to admit his failure to the Prince of Bakhtan.

"Despite all my desperate efforts," he said to him, his head bowed, "I am defeated. The Princess, Daughter of Happiness, is the victim of an evil spirit, a demon which is the cause of all her suffering and her pitiful condition. It has resisted all the spells and the most powerful charms that are known to the disciples of Thoth, the wise god. It is useless for me to bring more doctors and other magicians from the ends of the earth. This evil spirit will resist them just as it has resisted me. Only the god himself can deliver the Princess."

Then the Prince of Bakhtan decided to make a supreme effort to save Daughter of Happiness. There was no possibility of the invalid's being able to travel, so he sent to His Majesty the Pharaoh a third ambassador, who arrived in Thebes nine years after the first one.

The messenger presented himself before the sovereign in autumn and, like his predecessor, he found Rameses II at Thebes, in the process of celebrating the feast of Amon-Ra in the temple at Luxor.

"I come, O Majesty, to bring you the despairing plea of my master, the Prince of Bakhtan. He beseeches you to send someone to the aid of his daughter, the Princess Daughter of Happiness. He begs for the ultimate remedy for those in despair of their lives. Nothing can drive away the demon, which holds her in thrall, but the presence of the god himself who cures and saves. Consent, I beg you, to send the god Khons, the all-powerful, to the country of Bakhtan, so that he may drive away the evil which has tormented her for so long."

Before replying, Pharaoh entered the temple and penetrated into the chapel, where stood the statue of the god Khons, he who relieves all pains, because he is all-powerful over the spirits of evil.

Pharaoh prostrated himself at his feet, then, standing up, he offered up this prayer: "O my master, I throw myself at your feet once more on behalf of my father-in-law, the Prince of Bakhtan, who implores you to come to the aid of his daughter. O master, agree to transfer your powers to the statue and allow us to transport your image to the country of Bakhtan, and there, by your virtue, drive away the demon which tortures the sick Princess. Take healing and peace and tranquillity to the people of Bakhtan, who have worshipped you for so many years."

Twice, in succession, the god Khons bowed his head, at each part of Pharaoh's oration to show his approval and his acceptance. The statue nodded his head by the will of Khons. And the god introduced his power into the statue, his faithful image, so that it could be transported to the faraway country of Bakhtan.

The Pharaoh, Rameses II, gave orders which were promptly obeyed. The statue of the god was solemnly installed in a royal barge, escorted by five smaller barges, and a cortège of chariots and cavalry.

All along the way, the people of the towns and the villages worshipped the god and implored him to cure their ailments and to relieve their afflictions, and every day they offered up sacrifices.

The voyage, slowed up by these devotions, took seventeen months. Finally, when the convoy was approaching the country of Bakhtan, the Prince and all his court came to meet it, to welcome it with all the honours due to the gods, and with cries of joy and rejoicing.

The god was then carried into the Princess's apartments.

And the divine power which the god, Khons, had transferred into his image worked swiftly and miraculously: the Princess was delivered from her troubles immediately.

The demon, which had possessed her, left her body and addressed Khons: "Blessed, blessed are you, O great god, who drives away the demons and forbids them to torment men. Bakhtan belongs to you, all its people, men and women, are yours and I, myself, I am your slave. I am going to return to the place whence I came, and your heart can be reassured concerning the reason for your taking this long voyage. I implore you to order a great feast, at which I can rejoice with Your Majesty and with the Prince of Bakhtan."

The statue of the god inclined its head as a sign of agreement, and the priests of Khons arranged everything in collaboration with the Prince of Bakhtan. They organised great rejoicings to celebrate the departure of the evil spirit. The Prince of Bakhtan made an offering and a sacrifice to the god, Khons, and he did not forget the evil spirit. Then at the feet of the statue of Khons the Prince and the demon celebrated.

When the feasting was over, the evil spirit obeyed the orders of the god, Khons, and went back to his normal habitation, in the realm of Seth, without doubt. And the whole place rejoiced.

The Prince and all the people of Bakhtan were very well satisfied with this happy success. The Prince decided that he would like to think of the statue of the god, Khons, as a present and that he would never let it go back to Egypt.

So the statue remained in Bakhtan. But one night, at the end of three years and nine months, when the Prince was asleep in his bed, he had a vision. He saw the god, Khons, in the shape of a falcon who was leaving his sanctuary, soaring up into the sky and flying towards Egypt. When he awoke, he said to the priests of Khons: "The god who was sojourning with us has returned to Egypt; I must allow those who accompanied him to return also."

And the Prince sent back to Egypt the statue of the god with its cortège and its escort, and also many, many presents, as well as a guard of honour and soldiers and horses in great numbers.

After a long trek, the convoy reached Egypt and arrived at Thebes. The statue of the god, Khons, was put back in the Temple of Luxor at Thebes. And all the cases containing the gifts amassed on the way were also placed there.

Queen Neferu-Ra rejoiced in her heart to hear that the Daughter of Happiness was cured; and Pharaoh was happy because the Queen was satisfied.

13

The Story of Rampsinite

ONG ago, King Rampsinite possessed a large amount of treasure, so large that among his successors not even one has possessed more, nor for many years back had anyone accumulated so many riches.

Anxious to put his treasure out of the reach of robbers, and to guard it safely, he had a stone vault built at the side of the palace in such a way that one of the walls was accessible from outside. The mason who built the vault managed to place in this wall a well-mortared stone which was very close fitting and so well adjusted that two normal men, or even one man of great strength, could, without too much effort, lay hold of it, pull it out, and lift it from its place.

When the vault was completed, the King heaped it with all the riches of his treasure, satisfied to know that it was entirely safe.

Some time afterwards, the mason, feeling that the end

of his life was approaching, called his two sons to him and revealed to them how he had provided for their future by a skilful trick, and he told them how the King's vault had been constructed, so that they would be able to live in luxury.

After he had clearly explained the method of lifting out the stone, and the way to put it back in its place, and, after having strongly recommended certain precautions, he departed this life.

His children, naturally enough, lost no time in getting to work. They went out at night to roam around the King's palace. They easily found the stone in question, lifted it from its place, and took away a large sum of money. But fate decreed that the King should come to inspect his vault. He was very much astonished to find that the level of gold in his coffers had considerably fallen. He did not know whom to blame, whom to accuse, nor whom to suspect, for the seal which he, himself, had put upon the door was intact, the vault carefully closed and locked.

After returning there several times, he realised that the contents of the coffers continued to diminish. To stop the robbers from acting so freely, and from returning peacefully to their homes afterwards, he had some traps made and fixed near the coffers which contained his treasure.

The robbers arrived one fine night according to their usual custom, and one of them slipped into the vault, but suddenly, when he approached a coffer, he found himself caught in a trap.

Realising what terrible danger he was in, he called his brother, and advised him to come into the vault and cut off his head, so that it would be impossible to recognise him. Thus his brother would not be compromised and lost with him. The brother thought that the advice was good, so he immediately cut off his brother's head. Then he replaced the stone carefully, and returned home carrying the head with him.

When the day dawned, the King went into his vault. He was very frightened to see the body of the thief caught in the trap, without a head, and with no trace of anyone entering or leaving the vault.

Not knowing what was the best thing to do, he thought of hanging the body of the dead man on the town wall. He would have a watch kept upon it, and he would order the guards to bring before him anyone they saw weeping near the body or pitying the fate of the headless corpse.

When she saw that the body was thus exposed, the mother of the thief was deeply distressed, and ordered the surviving son to bring her the corpse of his brother. If he did not bring it, she threatened that she would go and find the King and tell him who had stolen the treasure.

The son knew his mother and knew, too, that she took things very much to heart, and that nothing would make her change her mind, however much he argued. So he thought things over and finally hit upon an idea.

He saddled some donkeys and loaded them with goatskins full of wine, and drove them before him. When he arrived near the guards, that is to say at the place where the body was hanging, he loosened two or three of the goatskins, and, at the sight of the wine running onto the ground, he uttered loud exclamations and beat his fists against his head, and altogether had the air of a man who did not know where to begin to repair the damage, nor to which of his donkeys he should turn first.

The guards, seeing this quantity of wine spreading over the ground, ran to help him, saying to themselves that to collect all this wine was enough gain in itself. The merchant behind the donkeys began to shout at them and pretended to be very angry. The guards were then very polite and agreeable to him; little by little he calmed down, and finally turned his donkeys off the road, so as to patch up the damage and load them again. Conversation went on about one thing and another. Talking about this and talking about that, one of the guards made a joke with the merchant, and the latter could not help laughing, and he ended by giving the guards a goatskin of wine. They lost no time in sitting down and beginning to drink. The merchant kept them company and, noting both their goodwill and their thirst, he gave them the rest of his load, and they drank the contents of all the goatskins. When they had finished it all, they were dead drunk, sleep took hold of them, and they all fell down where they were, without being able to move.

The merchant waited until the night was well advanced, then he cut down the corpse of his brother and, laughing at the guards in his turn, he shaved off all their beards on the right side of their cheeks. Then he put the body of his brother on the donkeys, drove them towards his home, and went in, having carried out his mother's orders.

The next day, when the King was told what had happened and he knew how the body of the thief had been skilfully removed, he was very angry. Wanting at all costs to find out who had outwitted him, he ordered one of his daughters, the Princess who was well known for her cunning, to find the guilty one. It was understood that she would bring the passers-by into the palace to talk with her, and that she would manage to make them say, by encouraging them to boast, the wisest and the wickedest thing that each one had done in his lifetime, and, if one of them told her the story of the thief, she must immediately seize him, and see that he did not get away.

The Princess obeyed, but the thief, hearing all about this, wanted to play an even cleverer trick on the King.

What could he think of this time? He cut off the arm of a man who had recently died and, hiding it under his robe, he strolled towards the palace. He visited the Princess and they were soon deep in conversation. Naturally, she put the same question to him as she had done to the others: "Tell me then what is the most cunning and the wickedest thing you have ever done in your life?"

He told her how his worst crime had been to cut off the head of his brother, who was caught in a trap in the King's vault, and that his most cunning action had been to make the guards drunk so as to cut down the body of his brother. As soon as the Princess realised to whom she was talking, she stretched out her hand, but the thief let her take the dead man's hand and, as she gripped it firmly, he slipped away. She realised that she had been tricked, and that he had had time to leave the palace and get right away. When this was told to the King, he was astonished, marvelling at the astuteness and courage of this man. He ordered it to be published throughout all the cities of his realm that he would pardon this thief, and that, if he would come forward and present himself to the King, he would give him great gifts. The thief was confident that this proclamation made by the King was a true one, so he went to see him.

When the King saw him, he judged him to be a rare bird and he gave him his daughter in marriage, as to the most cunning of men. Had he not, in fact, proof of the cunning of the Egyptians, who can outwit people of every nation?

14

The Scribe's Prophecy

T happened many years ago that there lived a poor peasant, who scarcely earned enough to buy his food. He was a linen merchant, who sold the peasants the rough cloth which he wove from the hemp he bought from them, and he made so little by these transactions that it was pitiful to see his penury.

He lived in the country in a little hovel, built of sunbaked mud, which had only one room. But there was a certain amount of land attached to it. This he had enclosed by means of a wall which he himself built, simply by placing one stone above another, so that he could have some privacy. The wall made a little courtyard in front of his dwelling and in the corner of this little courtyard—thanks to Amon-Ra—a fig-tree flourished. This fig-tree soon became a full-grown tree, and it was a great source of pleasure to the poor man. He used to rest under the shade of its large leaves, and when it produced figs he ate them with his bread. He never picked more than two a day during the season when they were ripe, so that they might last as long as possible; for, once they were over, he had to eat dry bread. In spite of his poverty, he worshipped Amon-Ra regularly, for he was a pious and virtuous man.

One year, during the winter, when he returned home after having sold his cloth, and when he turned towards the sun to say his prayers, he suddenly noticed that the fig-tree was covered with shining leaves and firm fruit. He counted ten figs on the branches, and one of them was enormous, round and purple, and so ripe that it seemed ready to drop and crush itself on the ground. The others, less big and less brightly-coloured, were ready to ripen one after another. The first action of the cloth merchant was to thank Amon-Ra, who had performed this miracle for his devoted servant; for here were figs to eat in midwinter! His second action, instead of picking the fig at once, in its perfect state, and enjoying it himself, was to go and consult his neighbour, a third-class scribe, who was much wiser than he.

This third-class scribe could read the future in the sand. He took the box where he kept his sand, smoothed it level, and traced some lines upon it. Then he made some complicated calculations in his head, uttered an incomprehensible magic formula, and finally said to the cloth merchant: "Every day, for ten successive days, you will take to Pharaoh the fig which is ripe and ready to eat on that particular day. On the tenth day, your destiny will be fulfilled. The good and the bad will be adjusted."

The cloth merchant could get nothing more out of him. He left a length of red linen as a token of gratitude and went home.

Now Pharaoh, in his magnificent palace at Luxor, went every morning to his Audience Hall as soon as the sun rose. Seated between the two great obelisks at the entrance of the great hall surrounded by his friends and his attendants, he listened to the complaints of his subjects with patience, and gave immediate judgment on the affairs they brought before him. No one, not even the most poverty-stricken, was turned away. At midday, Pharaoh returned to his palace and went into his harem, where he amused himself as he liked for the rest of the day.

The cloth merchant also rose up early in the morning. He was on the road before dawn, running towards Thebes, so as not to be the last, saying to himself: "The proverb says that in Egypt gold is the dust of the roads, but I see nothing beneath my feet but dust."

He slipped into the Audience Chamber, and took his place behind the line of plaintiffs who had, despite his efforts, arrived before him. He held a plate in his hand on which was displayed the beautiful ripe fig between two fringed napkins.

When his turn came, he prostrated himself before the throne of His Majesty, his nose in the dust; he touched his forehead and his ear with his right hand, whilst his left offered the plate to Pharaoh.

Without lifting his eyes to the sovereign, he said to him: "Oh my lord, sun of the skies, I, your servant, who am the dust at your feet and the soil that you tread, I roll in the dust on my stomach and on my back seven times at your feet. Behold, Amon-Ra, the great god, has shown favour unto me and sent me, upon my fig-tree and out of season, magnificent fruits that are large and ripe and

12

smelling delicious. It cannot be possible that such a god-
send is meant for the unworthy mouth of a poor merchant
like me. Certainly the god wishes to test me. It is fitting
that such rare things should be offered to Your Majesty,
for it is only you who are worthy of them. I have brought
you the first fig to ripen and, with your permission, I will
bring you the nine others each day as they are ready."

Pharaoh deigned to declare that the cloth merchant
had all the right sentiments to the highest degree, and he
approved of his actions. Better still, he admitted that for
some time he had been longing for fresh fruit. Finally, he
was so accommodating as to eat the fruit then and there.
He found it delicious, and said so.

Having appreciated the fig at its worth, ripe and sweet,
he called the palace steward, named Anzab, who was
standing behind him, and told him to give the poor cloth
merchant two cloaks of linen and a hundred pieces of
gold. The merchant went home very happy, draped in his
new robes. He lost no time in buying a white donkey to
carry his goods, and he invited his neighbours (without
forgetting the third-class scribe, who was the first to be
asked, and certainly deserved it) to come and feast with
him. He prepared an outstanding repast, consisting of
twenty roast geese, more than forty sweet dishes, good
beer, and even a pitcher of wine. None of them had ever
in their lives eaten so much or so well.

The next day the cloth merchant found that another
fig was ready and, without losing any time, he ran to take
it to His Majesty. The third fig was ripe the following day,
and so it continued. Each day the cloth merchant offered
the beautiful and rare fruit to His Majesty, and each day
also the present, which His Majesty gave him in return,

was even more valuable than that of the preceding day. Thus did the cloth merchant receive slaves, camels, lands, pieces of gold, and silver in quantities: so much so that the palace steward, who saw all these riches slipping away before his eyes, began to be very jealous.

"By the great god," said he in his heart. "If I do not take care, His Majesty is capable of driving me out and of giving my place to this poor individual, who is nothing but an intriguer."

When night fell, he went to the cloth merchant's dwelling, and he noticed that there only remained three figs upon the tree in the courtyard. He went into the house and saw the servants in the course of preparing a sumptuous feast: how life had changed for this wretch!

Anzab, the steward, hiding his envy, greeted the cloth merchant politely and paid him many flattering compliments. The greetings over, he added: "Assuredly, you are very much in favour at court! His Majesty is always talking about you. He has even thought about giving you the daughter of a general for your wife. But there is one difficulty in the way, one thing which holds back, your promotion. You must be in the habit of eating a great deal of garlic! His Majesty cannot bear the smell of garlic, so it would be a good idea if you were to hold a piece of white linen in front of your mouth when you come for a royal audience in the morning. Certainly Pharaoh would very much appreciate such a delicate attention and would reward you suitably."

The cloth merchant very much regretted having already eaten his fill of roast goose and leg of beef, prepared with garlic and garnished with a garlic sauce. The next morning when he went to present the best fig in the world (the eighth) to Pharaoh, he took care to envelop his neck and his mouth with a long white linen scarf.

He stood an arm's length away so as not to offend the susceptible nose of His Majesty. When the cloth merchant took his leave and had gone some distance, Pharaoh, intrigued, asked Anzab, the steward of the palace, what this unusual covering could mean.

"I do not know," replied Anzab, "but I will go and find out, so as to satisfy Your Majesty's curiosity."

Then he ran off, swiftly, oh so swiftly, as though he wanted to catch up the cloth merchant, but he returned with lagging steps, a disturbed look on his face, and his head bowed. More and more intrigued, Pharaoh questioned him. Anzab hesitated to answer, but finally Pharaoh gave him a definite order to speak.

As soon as Pharaoh began to get really angry, and when Anzab saw the hairs of the royal beard bristling, he decided, or rather pretended to decide, to speak in spite of himself. Prostrated upon the ground, he said in an ingratiating voice: "May Your Majesty forgive me, if I am obliged to repeat the dreadful suggestions made by this uncouth cloth merchant. This animal, this peasant of low birth, has no deference and no manners. He says that Your Majesty loads him with presents for which he is truly grateful, but that each time Your Majesty deigns to speak to him, you breathe into his face a nauseating puff of garlic which nearly makes him faint. He adds that he would never have believed that a Pharaoh could have bad breath unless he had proved it for himself. He winds the linen round his mouth so that he shall not smell it. If he did not, he would not be able to speak to Your Majesty without swooning."

"Behold," growled Pharaoh, "this wretch who finds that the breath of divine perfume is not good enough for his beastly nose." He was about to fly into a rage at the idea of this crime without precedent, when instead he burst out laughing: "That's good," he said, jokingly. "I shall not owe him anything. Let him come again and offer me his good fig, and I will show my gratitude in a way that will far outshine all my earlier presents to him."

Anzab, the steward of the palace, wondered whether he had not lost his chance and whether, in trying to ruin the prestige of the cloth merchant, he had not actually improved it. If Pharaoh, the King himself, was capable of valuing frankness above everything in the world, perhaps he, Anzab, had made a very great error, and one which would probably do him harm.

The next morning, the court saw the cloth merchant arrive, muffled up in his mask of white linen, his mouth well protected, the plate with the ripe fig in his hand.

Pharaoh took the fig and ate it greedily, and then looked at the merchant with a suspicious eye. Finally he asked for ink, a brush and papyrus. All the scribes rushed forward to offer their services. But Pharaoh pushed them aside with a gesture and, with his own hand, wrote quite a short letter, which he carefully sealed with his own insignia and gave to the cloth merchant, telling him to take this order to the Royal Treasury the next morning.

"You must ask for the Treasurer-in-Chief on my behalf and certainly you will not regret having done so."

The audience over, the palace steward, Anzab, accompanied the cloth merchant on his way and, while doing so, he congratulated him: "One can easily see that His

Majesty is very pleased with you," he hinted. "You did well to follow my advice. He has asked me to run after you to save you the trouble of going out of your way to the Treasury tomorrow morning. This order, written by Pharaoh's own hand, says that the Treasurer-in-Chief must count out a thousand pieces of silver in exchange for this letter sealed with the royal seal. His Majesty sent me to bring you these thousand pieces of gold. Here they are correctly counted in this sack. Give me the sealed order which is now useless."

The cloth merchant, delighted, took the sack and gave back the roll sealed with the royal insignia. Then he went on his way, and Anzab returned home. Anzab trembled with impatience all night, and the day had hardly dawned, when he was at the door of the Treasurer-in-Chief. The official took the roll, respectfully kissed the royal seal, broke it and read the letter. Immediately he raised his finger. Two soldiers of the guard came forward and seized Anzab, the palace steward. With one well-directed sweep of the sword, a third guard made his head fly into the air and drop on to the ground. The steward did not even have time to realise that all was over.

Meanwhile, the cloth merchant arrived as usual in the Audience Chamber, perfectly happy, his plate in his hand, his white scarf well wound round his neck and his mouth.

When he saw him, Pharaoh could not believe his eyes. He rubbed them vigorously and looked again: there was no doubt, the cloth merchant was there, very much alive and with his daily fig in his hand. Pharaoh then looked for the palace steward to ask for an explanation, but for the first time for years Anzab was not in his place. At that moment the Treasurer-in-Chief arrived, a big leather sack in his hand.

Pharaoh saw him and cried out: "Now then, why did you not obey my orders? Why did you not decapitate the man whom I sent to you with a roll written and sealed by my own hand?"

The Treasurer was already flat on the ground before Pharaoh, very much frightened.

"May Your Majesty forgive me. I cut him down as you ordered, conforming to the instructions in the letter he bore. Besides, see, here is his head."

And, opening the sack, he took out the head of the palace steward and laid it carefully at Pharaoh's feet. It would be impossible to describe the astonishment shown by everyone present in the Audience Chamber that morning.

"What," cried Pharaoh, "this is my palace steward, whose head you have cut off. This is terrible."

"But," replied the Treasurer-in-Chief, "Did not Your Majesty write with your own hand that, without further ceremony, I was to cut off the head of the bearer of this sealed letter? I obeyed without hesitating, instantly."

"Exactly," said Pharaoh. "But there has been a mistake. It was not the palace steward who was charged with bringing you the letter."

"This is certainly the man who brought me the letter, my master. I swear it."

The merchant, stupefied over it all, was taken aside and questioned. He recovered his wits sufficiently to tell how the palace steward had come to visit him in his house, to advise him to cover his mouth so that his unpleasant breath should not inconvenience His Majesty, and how this same Anzab had run after him to give him the thousand pieces of gold on behalf of Pharaoh, taking in exchange the roll sealed with the royal insignia.

Pharaoh had reached the limits of astonishment and surprise, and, not knowing what to say, praised Amon-Ra, the great god.

"Evidently," cried His Majesty, "this Anzab, the palace steward, is an old scoundrel, a wicked impostor, a lying traitor, an arrant thief, but all is well that ends well. If he has tricked everyone of us, if he wanted to steal, believing that I was going to load you with riches, and that the sealed order was worth a fortune, in his turn he has been robbed, and his head has paid for yours. But you shall take his place, and become the steward of my palace."

The cloth merchant bowed to the ground and his forehead touched the dust before the feet of Pharaoh. As he did so, His Majesty heard him murmur a few words.

"What are you mumbling about?" asked His Majesty. "Are you not satisfied?"

"I am overwhelmed with satisfaction, O my lord, but I am saying to myself that the third-class scribe saw the future very clearly. May he be blessed, for his learning is excellent."

"Who is this third-class scribe, and what has he to do with all this?" asked Pharaoh.

"Let Your Majesty see for himself. The day on which I consulted him, did he not advise me to offer my figs, which were so good and so beautiful, and too good for a poor peasant, to Pharaoh, alone worthy of eating such rarities, and did he not tell me that the tenth day, the good and the bad would find themselves each in his rightful place? Behold, the palace steward, Anzab, is dead and I, I have taken his place."

"All is well," said the Pharaoh. "But you have forgotten to give me the last fig." And His Majesty ate the tenth and last fig.

15

King Zeser in Distress

T the time of King Zeser, a pharaoh of the Third Dynasty, the viceroy of Nubia was a man named Meter. He was of noble birth and he lived in Elephantine. One of Meter's duties was to administer the properties belonging to the god Knemou.

Knemou was a very rich and powerful god and he was the master of the sources of the River Nile. Only his priests knew where these sources originated. They claimed that the Nile came from an abyss which had been carved out by the turbulent waters between two enormous pointed rocks which were called Crophi and Morphi. This ravine was so deep that it was impossible to plumb its depths even with the longest of ropes.

In the nineteenth year of his reign, the pharaoh Zeser sent a letter to the viceroy which read as follows:

"This letter is to inform you of the calamities which have befallen me since I ascended the throne, calamities which weigh as heavily on all my friends and all my subjects as they do on me.

"My heart is sad and I suffer great affliction. For the last seven seasons the waters of the Nile have not risen to their full height. For seven years we have seen no floods; the ground has remained dry and barren. It is nothing more than black mud dried in the sun; it is like a cracked crust from which no green thing sprouts. The trees are covered with dust, their leaves are enveloped in a thick, sticky coating. The harvest has produced no grain and the gardens are dried up. There is neither grass nor vegetation; all trace of nourishment has disappeared from the surface of the earth. The starving peasants steal from each other. These poor people all wish to seek their fortunes elsewhere but, weakened by their hunger, they lack even the strength to set out upon their journey. Little children groan and die; young people tremble with weakness. As for the old people, their hearts are broken with misery, their legs thrash out as they lie half-unconscious on the ground, holding their empty stomachs with their hands.

"The officials have no power to overcome the situation and know not what advice to give. When the public granaries are opened they are found to contain nothing but air. The whole kingdom is in ruins.

"I look back to the happy times, the times when I took good counsel. In those days the god sent us his great floods which made the country fertile each year. I used to see men and children paddling in the liquid mud, the cattle quenched their thirst, the insects swarmed above the surface of the water, birds swooped down to drink and forage for food and the fish Sabreka provided ample nourishment for hungry stomachs. Ah, that was the age of the gods, the age of Thoth the Ibis-god who fluttered above the waters, the time of the high priest Imoithis, the son of Thtah. In those days everything was prosperous. Both my subjects and my friends who lived close to me in the Great House were surrounded by abundance.

"I beg of you, send me the information I require. Where is the source of the Nile? Which god is master of it? What do you know of this god? Tell me all, since our lives depend upon it. It is he who piles up the grain in our granaries; if he does not bless us once again, we shall all perish.

"I am anxious to consult the high priest of Thoth at Hermopolis. His blessing fortifies mankind and supports them in their despair. I wish to gain entrance to the library of the Temple of Memphis, to the House of Life. I wish to seize the rolls of papyrus with my own hands and to decipher the writings which cover them. I wish to read the sacred books, to meditate on them and to discover the significance of all the mysteries they contain."

When the viceroy Meter had read this royal letter with great care, he hastened to set out on his journey to rejoin the Pharaoh. As soon as he was by his side, he began to instruct the King. He replied, as far as he was able, to the questions His Majesty had posed and gave him information on the source of the Nile. He recounted to him the views of wise men who had written theses on this subject. Then he took up the relevant books and read all the important passages to the King, helping him to decipher any difficult sections and explaining to him some passages which appeared obscure. All this was necessary since the Pharaoh's ancestors had only consulted these books hastily. Since the distant days when Ra himself had ruled over Egypt, these matters had never been studied with care or explained to any of the kings. Indeed, there was hardly need for this since the Nile had never known drought.

Then the viceroy Meter said to the Pharaoh, "There is a town on the river from which the Nile seems to draw its very existence. It is an ancient town which goes back to the beginning of the world and it is called Abou. It is known as the City of the Beginning and it is there—far, far away to the south—that we find the part of the world which was created before all others. There, there is a great sequence of steps, a staircase in fact, and it is there that the Lord Ra rested when he had created the first men. There are two caverns there from which spring the two rivers which are said to be the sources of the Nile. All the prosperity of Egypt depends on that spot. The great floods which irrigate our lands originate there. There the water rises to a height four times greater than at Hermopolis.

"This is how it happens. The god of the Nile rises, rejuvenated by his long rest in the caverns where he has regained all his strength. He paces along the sand, he draws the bolts and opens wide the two flood-gates which allow the water to escape. The river flows in full spate and soon the fields and gardens of the whole kingdom are covered with vegetation and men rejoice at the idea of the harvest which is to come.

"The god of the Nile is known by the name of Shou. He keeps account of all the produce of Egypt, in order to check that each person has his fair share. It is he who measures the fields and keeps a register of the various territories. He lives in a house which faces towards the south-east, and its door is made of reeds, while its roof is formed from the branches of trees. Round about are the mountains and the quarries to which the stone-masons go with their tools to seek out stone for the construction of temples for the gods, palaces for the sacred animals, statues and pyramids for the dead. This, indeed, is the stone of Abou which never crumbles. In the sanctuary, pious men offer sacrifices to the gods and sweet perfumes are presented to the god Knemou, to Osiris, to Isis, to Horus and to Nephthys.

"In the secret chambers with sealed entrances there are piles of treasure—precious stones, gold and silver, bronze and iron, lapis lazuli, emerald, crystal, rubies and alabaster. Here too, are seeds of the plants which produce incense and all other things which grateful men offer each autumn to the gods who have granted them such favours."

Thus the viceroy Meter expounded to the Pharaoh the essential aspects of life in his kingdom and it was then that Pharaoh decided to make a personal pilgrimage to the temple of Knemou.

There, having prayed, he fell asleep. In his dream he saw the god and addressed him thus:

"I entered the temple, the guardian of the books untied the cords which held them and unrolled them for me so that I could see their contents.

"I was purified by being sprinkled with holy water and I entered into the secret parts of the temple where no one has ever been admitted previously.

"Here, in gratitude, I have made my offering to the gods and goddesses of the city of Abou. I have given them cakes and beer, geese and oxen.

"And then I saw the god Knemou standing before me

and tried to explain my plight to him and to gain his sympathy by making him great gifts. I prayed to him and I begged him to listen to our cries.

"He deigned to move his eyelids and to show his sympathy. From the height of his majestic grandeur, he let fall these words.

"'I am Knemou, the god of creation. With my two hands I gathered up the earth and fashioned the body of man as he is and as you are. I gave you your limbs and I fashioned your heart.

"'But still man lacks gratitude. The stones which should have been cut for the construction of my temple still lie in the quarry, in the depths of the earth. No attempt has been made to repair the holy resting-places of the gods; they have crumbled in dust and in ruins.

"'It seems that men and kings are unaware of the fact that I, the Creator, the All-powerful, and the Master who has given them health and life, am the greatest, the father of all the gods and ruler of the whole world. The two halves of the heavens are my dwelling-place. It is I who pour the waters of the Nile so that the river can flood the ploughed fields and irrigate them, so that it can give life to all those who live within the flooded areas.

"'I shall make the waters of the Nile rise for you; there shall no longer be years of drought. The river will flow and the waters will cover the fields and bring joy to all your people. The plants and the grasses will flourish. Stalks will bend under the weight of the grain. Trees will bow under burden of their fruits—the fig-tree, the pomegranate-tree and the apricot-tree will all flourish. The fruit of the lotus will burst and release its seeds from which a delectable cake will be made for you, O Pharaoh.

" 'The goddess of the harvest will preside and on all sides the harvest will be seven thousand times more abundant. For each year the waters will rise higher and higher and go further and further.

" 'Your people will be overwhelmed with produce. Each one will receive much more than he desires. Hunger will disappear and people will no longer contemplate empty granaries. All Egypt will be cultivated. The fields will be yellow with ripening corn and the ears will be full. The whole kingdom will be so fertile that it will surpass the hopes of the fellahin and far exceed anything known before.' "

At this hopeful promise of abundant harvest, the King awoke and courage and hope flourished in his heart to replace the despair which had lodged there for so long.

And since the time of that bond between the god Knemou and the Pharaoh, the Nile has never ceased to send a flood of green waters in the spring followed by a flood of red waters. For three whole months the earth absorbs the fertile moisture. Meadows laugh, banks flower, men are happy in anticipation of a good harvest. Every stomach rejoices and every tooth is sharpened thanks to the gift of the Nile which men revere and adore as the lord of health-giving nourishment.